MW01131656

THE
Shawl Society

SEASON 1

Six shawl knitting patterns
to delight and inspire

HELEN STEWART

CURIOUS HANDMADE

HELEN STEWART

THE SHAWL SOCIETY SEASON 1

Six shawl knitting patterns to delight and inspire

Published by Curious Handmade Ltd

www.curioushandmade.com

© Helen Stewart, 2018

All rights reserved.

All Shawl photography by Vicki Hillman
Contents image Charisse Kenion on Unsplash
Shawl Society image by Samuel Ferrara on Unsplash

No part of this publication may be reproduced, stored in a retrieval system, or transmitted
in any form or by any means – electronic, mechanical, photocopy, recording, or any
other without the prior written permission of the publisher.

Purchasing this book allows you to use it for personal, non-commercial purposes.

Items produced using the directions in this book are not licensed to be sold.

ISBN 978-1-9993409-0-2

Contents

The patterns in this book were the
starting point for heart-warming
conversations, generous sharing
of knowledge and know-how, and
thousands of breathtaking finished
shawls from inspired
Shawl Society members.

Welcome to Curious Handmade

By buying this book you've been initiated into a close-knit community of intrepid knitters from around the globe. If it all seems a little mysterious, that's as it should be. Let me explain...

The idea for the Shawl Society first arose several years ago. I was thinking a lot about what I could do to delight the Curious Crew (my affectionate name for the group of fabulous knitters who make such beautiful things from my patterns). After a lot of soul-searching, brainstorming, and talking to knitters about their goals and dreams, the concept of the Shawl Society was born. I was delighted with the idea of a series of mystery shawl patterns. Shawls were, and are, my favourite thing to design, and I always love the joyful anticipation of a surprise. I hoped that the knitters would agree!

As it turns out, they did.

The first season of The Shawl Society caught the imaginations of knitters from all over the world. These brave souls jumped into the unknown together and took on the challenge of six mystery shawls, sight unseen. The patterns in this book were the starting point for heart-warming conversations, generous sharing of knowledge and know-how, and thousands of breathtaking finished shawls from inspired Shawl Society members. The designs were originally revealed one by one over the course of six months, but now you have the opportunity to enjoy them all at once. The response to the first Shawl Society was so overwhelming that I decided to gather the patterns into this book you now hold in your hands, as a memento for those who were there at the beginning, and as a way to invite even more knitters into the joy of knitting these shawls.

This first Shawl Society collection has a boho theme, embodying the cornerstone of the Curious Handmade style. Romantic and timeless, but with a distinctly modern edge, each of these shawls holds a very special place in my heart. I hope they find their way into yours, too.

Happy knitting!

Helen

THE

Shawl
Society

SEASON 1

When I was designing this collection,
I wanted it to be a true representation
of the Curious Handmade aesthetic.
As a designer, I'm an incurable romantic,
and that certainly comes out in my patterns.

What I love best of all is to incorporate the beautiful and bohemian into a modern design sensibility. That's how I approached each of these shawl patterns. A bit of lovely lace, a dainty edging, delicate eyelets: all those little vintage-inspired details to make your heart sing, but with clean lines and sophisticated textures.

I also wanted to make sure that there was plenty of variety in the collection to keep things interesting. You'll discover shawls in a wide variety of shapes, yarn weights, fibres, and colour combinations. It's important to me that my designs are as fun to make as they are to wear, so I created them to be within reach for an adventurous beginner knitter, with enough interest and challenge to keep the experts engaged the whole way through.

I've added in lots of helpful bits at the end of the book. You'll find more information about using the special Curious Handmade Percentage Checklist System™ pattern format, advice on choosing yarn for your projects, and some useful techniques for knitting your shawls. For a little extra help and a peek behind the scenes, you can access my bonus videos at www.curioushandmade. com/TSS1bonus.

Even now, several years after the original knit-alongs, the community remains a big part of the Shawl Society experience. If you ever run into a challenge and need some advice, or if you've completed a shawl that you just have to show off, there are thousands of Shawl Society members on Instagram and Ravelry who would love to get to know you. And as always, the Curious Handmade support team is just an email away too.

Magical, safe, and full of good fortune, Talisman is a carefree crescent shawl, inscribed with a simple star stitch. Traditional lore advises that a talisman should always be made by the hands of the one who intends to use it.

By my reckoning that makes this shawl perfect for some selfish knitting. These cherished objects were often made to protect pilgrims on their journey, and it just so happens that Talisman makes wonderful travel knitting.

The pattern has been designed to showcase beautiful hand dyed yarn: subtly tonal, boldly variegated or a tranquil gradient, and it includes three versatile sizes. The small is a one skein project, ideal for crafting a special yarn into something charmed. The large size is just right for two skeins of fingering yarn or a beautiful laceweight.

Above Size: Small   Yarn: The Wool Kitchen Urban Hints Collection
Left Size: Medium   Yarn: Northbound Knitting BFL Silk Fingering

Size: Small   Yarn: The Wool Kitchen Urban Hints Collection

Size: Small   Yarn: The Wool Kitchen Urban Hints Collection

SPECIFICATIONS

SIZE

Small, Medium, Large

FINISHED MEASUREMENTS

Small

Approximately 137cm (54") diameter across straight top edge
38cm (15") neck to bottom edge

Medium

Approximately 168cm (66") diameter across straight top edge
43cm (17") neck to bottom edge

Large

Approximately 188cm (74") diameter across straight top edge
51cm (20") neck to bottom edge

YARN

Small

The Wool Kitchen Urban Hints Collection [50% Merino, 50% Silk, 400m/437yds per 100g skein], 1 x 100g skein, Colourway: Worn Denim (blue sample) Happy Hour (pink sample)

OR
100g of fingering or sock weight yarn totalling approximately 400m/437yds

Medium

Northbound Knitting BFL Silk Fingering [55% Superwash BFL, 45% Silk, 400m/437yds per 100g skein], 1.5 x 100g skein, Colourway: Verdigris
OR
150g of fingering or sock weight yarn totalling approximately 600m/656yds

Large

Northbound Knitting BFL Silk Fingering [55% Superwash BFL, 45% Silk, 400m/437yds per 100g skein], 2 x 100g skein, Colourway: Beaches
OR
200g of fingering or sock weight yarn totalling approximately 800m/874yds
OR
100g of lace weight yarn totalling approximately 800m/874yds

NEEDLES

Fingering/sock weight yarn

3.75mm (US 5), circular needles (any length)
4mm (US 6), 80/100cm (32/40") long circular needles (or size to obtain gauge)

Lace weight yarn

3.5mm (US 4), circular needles (any length)
3.75mm (US 5), 80/100cm (32/40") long circular needles (or size to obtain gauge)

NOTIONS

Tapestry needle

GAUGE

22 sts/28 rows = 10cm (4") in stockinette stitch after blocking

TALISMAN NOTES

This shawl is knit from the top down.

I recommend casting on and knitting the first 14 rows on smaller needles to create a smoother line across the top of the shawl.

Note that unless otherwise stated, every RS row is as written in row 7 and every WS row is as written in row 8.

The shawl is crescent in shape and increases are made at the edges. Two stitches are increased each

RS edge (4 sts increased each RS row in total) and one stitch is increased each WS edge (2 sts increased each WS row in total).

The percentages given are calculated based on the percentage of total stitches in the shawl. This can help guide you regarding how much yarn you need. E.g. if you weigh your yarn at the beginning and then at 10%, it will give you an indication of how much yarn you will need in total.

Pay special attention to the border stitches throughout the shawl. The KYOK stitch is tricky to fix after you have passed that row so pay careful attention to whether you are on a RS row working a KYOK or a WS row working a YO.

The border is both written out and charted so you can choose whichever you prefer to follow.

Size: Medium Yarn: Northbound Knitting BFL Silk Fingering

Size: Large Yarn: Northbound Knitting BFL Silk Fingering

Small

ROW	DIRECTIONS	TOTAL STITCHES	% DONE
	With 3.75mm (US5) needles, cast on 5 sts, using backward loop method	5	
1	[RS] Knit	5	
2	[WS] Knit	5	
3	[RS] K1, kfb, k1, kfb, k1	7	
4	[WS] K2, [yo, k1] four times, k1	11	
5	[RS] K3, KYOK, k3, KYOK, k3	15	
6	[WS] K2, p1, yo, purl to last 3 sts, yo, p1, k2	17	
7	[RS] K3, KYOK, knit to last 4 sts, KYOK, k3 (and all following RS rows unless otherwise stated)	21	
8	[WS] K2, p1, yo, purl to last 3 sts, yo, p1, k2 (and all following WS rows unless otherwise stated)	23	
9	[RS]	27	
10	[WS]	29	
11	[RS]	33	
12	[WS]	35	
13	[RS]	39	
14	[WS]	41	
15	[RS] Change to 4mm (US6) needles	45	
16	[WS]	47	
17	[RS]	51	
18	[WS]	53	
19	[RS]	57	
20	[WS]	59	
21	[RS]	63	
22	[WS]	65	
23	[RS]	69	
24	[WS]	71	
25	[RS]	75	
26	[WS]	77	
27	[RS]	81	5%

ROW	DIRECTIONS	TOTAL STITCHES	% DONE
28	[WS]	83	
29	[RS] K3, KYOK, K6, *STAR, K3* to last 13 sts, STAR, K6, KYOK, k3	87	
30	[WS]	89	
31	[RS]	93	
32	[WS]	95	
33	[RS]	99	
34	[WS]	101	
35	[RS]	105	
36	[WS]	107	
37	[RS]	111	
38	[WS]	113	10%
39	[RS]	117	
40	[WS]	119	
41	[RS]	123	
42	[WS]	125	
43	[RS]	129	
44	[WS]	131	
45	[RS] K3, KYOK, K9, *STAR, K3* to last 16 sts, STAR, K9, KYOK, k3	135	
46	[WS]	137	15%
47	[RS]	141	
48	[WS]	143	
49	[RS]	147	
50	[WS]	149	
51	[RS]	153	
52	[WS]	155	
53	[RS]	159	
54	[WS]	161	20%
55	[RS]	165	
56	[WS]	167	
57	[RS]	171	
58	[WS]	173	
59	[RS]	177	
60	[WS]	179	25%

ROW	DIRECTIONS	TOTAL STITCHES	% DONE
61	[RS] K3, KYOK, K6, *STAR, K3* to last 13 sts, STAR, K6, KYOK, k3	183	
62	[WS]	185	
63	[RS]	189	
64	[WS]	191	
65	[RS]	195	
66	[WS]	197	30%
67	[RS]	201	
68	[WS]	203	
69	[RS]	207	
70	[WS]	209	
71	[RS]	213	35%
72	[WS]	215	
73	[RS]	219	
74	[WS]	221	
75	[RS]	225	
76	[WS]	227	40%
77	[RS] K3, KYOK, K9, *STAR, K3* to last 16 sts, STAR, K9, KYOK, k3	231	
78	[WS]	233	
79	[RS]	237	
80	[WS]	239	45%
81	[RS]	243	
82	[WS]	245	
83	[RS]	249	
84	[WS]	251	
85	[RS]	255	50%
86	[WS]	257	
87	[RS]	261	
88	[WS]	263	
89	[RS]	267	55%
90	[WS]	269	
91	[RS]	273	
92	[WS]	275	
93	[RS] K3, KYOK, K6, *STAR, K3* to last 13 sts, STAR, K6, KYOK, k3	279	60%

ROW	DIRECTIONS	TOTAL STITCHES	% DONE
94	[WS]	281	
95	[RS]	285	
96	[WS]	287	
97	[RS]	291	65%
98	[WS]	293	
99	[RS]	297	
100	[WS]	299	70%
101	[RS]	303	
102	[WS]	305	
103	[RS]	309	
104	[WS]	311	75%
105	[RS]	315	
106	[WS]	317	
107	[RS]	321	80%
108	[WS]	323	
109	[RS] **Border:** K3, KYOK, K3, *STAR, K3* to last 10 sts, STAR, K3, KYOK, k3	327	
110	[WS]	329	85%
111	[RS]	333	
112	[WS]	335	
113	[RS] K3, KYOK, K6, *yo, K3* to last 7 sts, K3, KYOK, k3	445	90%
114	[WS]	447	
115	[RS] K3, KYOK, K10, *yo, S2KP, yo, K5* to last 9 sts, K5, KYOK, k3	451	
116	[WS]	453	95%
117	**Picot Cast Off:** Cast off 9 sts,*slip st back onto left needle, cast on 3 sts using knitted cast on method, cast off 11 sts* repeat to last 11sts, cast on 3 sts using knitted cast on method, cast off final 14 sts		100%

Medium

ROW	DIRECTIONS	TOTAL STITCHES	% DONE
	With 3.75mm (US5) needles, cast on 5 sts, using backward loop method	5	
1	[RS] Knit	5	
2	[WS] Knit	5	
3	[RS] K1, kfb, k1, kfb, k1	7	
4	[WS] K2, [yo, k1] four times, k1	11	
5	[RS] K3, KYOK, k3, KYOK, k3	15	
6	[WS] K2, p1, yo, purl to last 3 sts, yo, p1, k2	17	
7	[RS] K3, KYOK, knit to last 4 sts, KYOK, k3 (and all following RS rows unless otherwise stated)	21	
8	[WS] K2, p1, yo, purl to last 3 sts, yo, p1, k2 (and all following WS rows unless otherwise stated)	23	
9	[RS]	27	
10	[WS]	29	
11	[RS]	33	
12	[WS]	35	
13	[RS]	39	
14	[WS]	41	
15	[RS] Change to 4mm (US6) needles	45	
16	[WS]	47	
17	[RS]	51	
18	[WS]	53	
19	[RS]	57	
20	[WS]	59	
21	[RS]	63	
22	[WS]	65	
23	[RS]	69	
24	[WS]	71	
25	[RS]	75	
26	[WS]	77	
27	[RS]	81	
28	[WS]	83	
29	[RS] K3, KYOK, K6, *STAR, K3* to last 13 sts, STAR, K6, KYOK, k3	87	
30	[WS]	89	5%

ROW	DIRECTIONS	TOTAL STITCHES	% DONE
31	[RS]	93	
32	[WS]	95	
33	[RS]	99	
34	[WS]	101	
35	[RS]	105	
36	[WS]	107	
37	[RS]	111	
38	[WS]	113	
39	[RS]	117	
40	[WS]	119	
41	[RS]	123	
42	[WS]	125	
43	[RS]	129	10%
44	[WS]	131	
45	[RS] K3, KYOK, K9, *STAR, K3* to last 16 sts, STAR, K9, KYOK, k3	135	
46	[WS]	137	
47	[RS]	141	
48	[WS]	143	
49	[RS]	147	
50	[WS]	149	
51	[RS]	153	
52	[WS]	155	
53	[RS]	159	15%
54	[WS]	161	
55	[RS]	165	
56	[WS]	167	
57	[RS]	171	
58	[WS]	173	
59	[RS]	177	
60	[WS]	179	
61	[RS] K3, KYOK, K6, *STAR, K3* to last 13 sts, STAR, K6, KYOK, k3	183	20%
62	[WS]	185	
63	[RS]	189	
64	[WS]	191	
65	[RS]	195	
66	[WS]	197	
67	[RS]	201	

ROW	DIRECTIONS	TOTAL STITCHES	% DONE
68	[WS]	203	25%
69	[RS]	207	
70	[WS]	209	
71	[RS]	213	
72	[WS]	215	
73	[RS]	219	
74	[WS]	221	30%
75	[RS]	225	
76	[WS]	227	
77	[RS] K3, KYOK, K9, *STAR, K3* to last 16 sts, STAR, K9, KYOK, k3	231	
78	[WS]	233	
79	[RS]	237	
80	[WS]	239	35%
81	[RS]	243	
82	[WS]	245	
83	[RS]	249	
84	[WS]	251	
85	[RS]	255	
86	[WS]	257	40%
87	[RS]	261	
88	[WS]	263	
89	[RS]	267	
90	[WS]	269	
91	[RS]	273	45%
92	[WS]	275	
93	[RS] K3, KYOK, K6, *STAR, K3* to last 13 sts, STAR, K6, KYOK, k3	279	
94	[WS]	281	
95	[RS]	285	
96	[WS]	287	50%
97	[RS]	291	
98	[WS]	293	
99	[RS]	297	
100	[WS]	299	
101	[RS]	303	55%
102	[WS]	305	
103	[RS]	309	
104	[WS]	311	

ROW	DIRECTIONS	TOTAL STITCHES	% DONE
105	[RS]	315	60%
106	[WS]	317	
107	[RS]	321	
108	[WS]	323	
109	[RS] K3, KYOK, K9, *STAR, K3* to last 16 sts, STAR, K9, KYOK, k3	327	65%
110	[WS]	329	
111	[RS]	333	
112	[WS]	335	
113	[RS]	339	70%
114	[WS]	341	
115	[RS]	345	
116	[WS]	347	
117	[RS]	351	75%
118	[WS]	353	
119	[RS]	357	
120	[WS]	359	
121	[RS]	363	80%
122	[WS]	365	
123	[RS]	369	
124	[WS]	371	
125	[RS] **Border:** K3, KYOK, K6, *STAR, K3* to last 13 sts, STAR, K6, KYOK, k3	375	85%
126	[WS]	377	
127	[RS]	381	
128	[WS]	383	
129	[RS] K3, KYOK, K9, *yo, K3* to last 10 sts, K6, KYOK, k3	507	90%
130	[WS]	509	
131	[RS] K3, KYOK, K13, *yo, S2KP, yo, K5* to last 12 sts, K8, KYOK, k3	513	95%
132	[WS]	515	
	Picot Cast Off: Cast off 12 sts,*slip st back onto left needle, cast on 3 sts using knitted cast on method, cast off 11 sts* repeat to last 14sts, cast on 3 sts using knitted cast on method, cast off final 17 sts		100%

Large

ROW	DIRECTIONS	TOTAL STITCHES	% DONE
	Fingering weight yarn: With 3.75mm (US5) needles, cast on 5 sts, using backward loop method **Lace weight yarn:** With 3.5mm (US4) needles, cast on 5 sts, using backward loop method	5	
1	[RS] Knit	5	
2	[WS] Knit	5	
3	[RS] K1, kfb, k1, kfb, k1	7	
4	[WS] K2, [yo, k1] four times, k1	11	
5	[RS] K3, KYOK, k3, KYOK, k3	15	
6	[WS] K2, p1, yo, purl to last 3 sts, yo, p1, k2	17	
7	[RS] K3, KYOK, knit to last 4 sts, KYOK, k3 **(and all following RS rows unless otherwise stated)**	21	
8	[WS] K2, p1, yo, purl to last 3 sts, yo, p1, k2 **(and all following WS rows unless otherwise stated)**	23	
9	[RS]	27	
10	[WS]	29	
11	[RS]	33	
12	[WS]	35	
13	[RS]	39	
14	[WS]	41	
15	[RS] **Fingering weight yarn:** Change to 4mm (US6) needles **Lace weight yarn:** Change to 3.75mm (US5) needles	45	
16	[WS]	47	
17	[RS]	51	
18	[WS]	53	
19	[RS]	57	
20	[WS]	59	
21	[RS]	63	
22	[WS]	65	
23	[RS]	69	
24	[WS]	71	
25	[RS]	75	
26	[WS]	77	
27	[RS]	81	
28	[WS]	83	
29	[RS] K3, KYOK, K6, *STAR, K3* to last 13 sts, STAR, K6, KYOK, k3	87	

ROW	DIRECTIONS	TOTAL STITCHES	% DONE
30	[WS]	89	
31	[RS]	93	
32	[WS]	95	
33	[RS]	99	
34	[WS]	101	5%
35	[RS]	105	
36	[WS]	107	
37	[RS]	111	
38	[WS]	113	
39	[RS]	117	
40	[WS]	119	
41	[RS]	123	
42	[WS]	125	
43	[RS]	129	
44	[WS]	131	
45	[RS] K3, KYOK, K9, *STAR, K3* to last 16 sts, STAR, K9, KYOK, k3	135	
46	[WS]	137	
47	[RS]	141	
48	[WS]	143	10%
49	[RS]	147	
50	[WS]	149	
51	[RS]	153	
52	[WS]	155	
53	[RS]	159	
54	[WS]	161	
55	[RS]	165	
56	[WS]	167	
57	[RS]	171	
58	[WS]	173	
59	[RS]	177	15%
60	[WS]	179	
61	[RS] K3, KYOK, K6, *STAR, K3* to last 13 sts, STAR, K6, KYOK, k3	183	
62	[WS]	185	
63	[RS]	189	
64	[WS]	191	
65	[RS]	195	
66	[WS]	197	
67	[RS]	201	
68	[WS]	203	
69	[RS]	207	20%
70	[WS]	209	
71	[RS]	213	
72	[WS]	215	

ROW	DIRECTIONS	TOTAL STITCHES	% DONE
73	[RS]	219	
74	[WS]	221	
75	[RS]	225	
76	[WS]	227	25%
77	[RS] K3, KYOK, K9, *STAR, K3* to last 16 sts, STAR, K9, KYOK, k3	231	
78	[WS]	233	
79	[RS]	237	
80	[WS]	239	
81	[RS]	243	
82	[WS]	245	
83	[RS]	249	30%
84	[WS]	251	
85	[RS]	255	
86	[WS]	257	
87	[RS]	261	
88	[WS]	263	
89	[RS]	267	
90	[WS]	269	35%
91	[RS]	273	
92	[WS]	275	
93	[RS] K3, KYOK, K6, *STAR, K3* to last 13 sts, STAR, K6, KYOK, k3	279	
94	[WS]	281	
95	[RS]	285	
96	[WS]	287	40%
97	[RS]	291	
98	[WS]	293	
99	[RS]	297	
100	[WS]	299	
101	[RS]	303	
102	[WS]	305	45%
103	[RS]	309	
104	[WS]	311	
105	[RS]	315	
106	[WS]	317	
107	[RS]	321	50%
108	[WS]	323	
109	[RS] K3, KYOK, K9, *STAR, K3* to last 16 sts, STAR, K9, KYOK, k3	327	
110	[WS]	329	
111	[RS]	333	
112	[WS]	335	
113	[RS]	339	55%
114	[WS]	341	

ROW	DIRECTIONS	TOTAL STITCHES	% DONE
115	[RS]	345	
116	[WS]	347	
117	[RS]	351	
118	[WS]	353	60%
119	[RS]	357	
120	[WS]	359	
121	[RS]	363	
122	[WS]	365	65%
123	[RS]	369	
124	[WS]	371	
125	[RS] K3, KYOK, K6, *STAR, K3* to last 13 sts, STAR, K6, KYOK, k3	375	
126	[WS]	377	
127	[RS]	381	70%
128	[WS]	383	
129	[RS]	387	
130	[WS]	389	
131	[RS]	393	
132	[WS]	395	75%
133	[RS]	399	
134	[WS]	401	
135	[RS]	405	
136	[WS]	407	80%
137	[RS]	411	
138	[WS]	413	
139	[RS]	417	
140	[WS]	419	85%
141	[RS] **Border:** K3, KYOK, K3, *STAR, K3* to last 10 sts, STAR, K3, KYOK, k3	423	
142	[WS]	425	
143	[RS]	429	
144	[WS]	431	90%
145	[RS] K3, KYOK, K6, *yo, K3* to last 7 sts, K3, KYOK, k3	573	
146	[WS]	575	
147	[RS] K3, KYOK, K10, *yo, S2KP, yo, K5* to last 9 sts, K5, KYOK, k3	579	95%
148	[WS]	581	
	Picot Cast Off: Cast off 9 sts,*slip st back onto left needle, cast on 3 sts using knitted cast on method, cast off 11 sts* repeat to last 11sts, cast on 3 sts using knitted cast on method, cast off final 14 sts		100%

Charts

Charts are read from bottom to top. They are read right to left on right side rows, and left to right on wrong side rows. Row numbers corresponding to the written directions are displayed to the right of each chart.

CHART KEY

☐	knit on right side, purl on wrong side
☐•	purl on right side, knit on wrong side
O	yo
Ⅴ	KYOK
λ	S2KP
☒	STAR
▨	no stitch
☐	pattern repeat

Size: Small Yarn: The Wool Kitchen Urban Hints Collection

SMALL

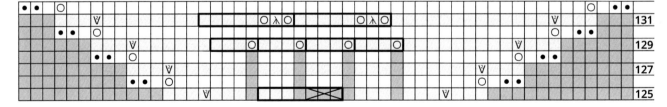

MEDIUM

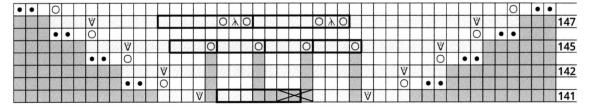

LARGE

FINISHING

Weave in ends.

BLOCKING

For detailed blocking instructions see page 82.

Size: Large Yarn: Northbound Knitting BFL Silk Fingering

AMULET

Shawl

Amulet was inspired by the mystical beauty of an ancient Egyptian carving of a powerful scarab beetle with wings outstretched to provide shelter and protection from harm. The elongated triangle shape of this shawl recalls the scarab's wings, which are also echoed in the graphically striking rib section.

The most important characteristic of any amulet is the power ascribed to it by its owner, and I have tried to infuse this design with some of that energy and intention. The sacred significance of handmade objects is something that every knitter knows. Made for yourself, it is an eloquent act of self-care. When knit for a loved one, it is a compelling symbol of comfort and love.

Featuring lace, eyelets, and optional beading (for a little extra magic), the Amulet shawl pattern offers two sizes: medium and large. With plenty of intriguing details to keep you interested, this is an exciting knit that is also well within the reach of courageous new shawl knitters. It can be knit in one, two, or even more colours, making it an excellent project for stash busting.

Left and above Size: Large Yarn: Madelinetosh Tosh Merino Light

Size: Medium Yarn: Seven Sisters Arts – Matrika

SPECIFICATIONS

SIZE

Medium, Large

FINISHED MEASUREMENTS

Medium

152cm (60") diameter across
top edge
51cm (20") neck to bottom edge

Large

178cm (70") diameter across
top edge
66cm (26") neck to bottom edge

YARN

Medium

Seven Sisters Arts – Matrika [80%
superwash merino, 20% silk,
365m/400yds per 100g skein],
2 x 100g skeins,
Main Colour: Damselfly
Contrast Colour: Nickel

OR

Approximately 160g of fingering
or sock weight yarn totalling
approximately 585m/640yds

If knitting the medium in two colours
you will need approximately 80g of
each colour

Large

Madelinetosh Tosh Merino Light
[100% Merino, 384m/420yds
per 100g skein], 2 x 100g skeins,
Colour: Sand Dune

OR

Approximately 200g of fingering
yarn totalling approximately
768m/840yds

If knitting the large in two colours you
will need one whole 100g skein of
each colour

NEEDLES

4mm (US 6), 100cm (40") long
circular needles (or size to obtain
gauge)
3.75mm (US 5), 80/100cm
(32/40") long circular needles
(or size to obtain gauge)

NOTIONS

Tapestry needle
1 Stitch marker
If using beads (optional)
US Steel Size 12/1.0mm Crochet
hook (or hook small enough to fit
through holes in beads)

Medium

Approx. 480 beads / 40g size 6
seed beads (beads used in sample
are Miyuki beads)

Large

Approx. 600 beads / 50g size 6
seed beads

GAUGE

19 sts/34 rows = 10cm (4") in
garter stitch after blocking

AMULET NOTES

When planning your shawl you can choose any combination of:

- Medium or Large

- One or two colours (or you could even do more than two colours if you are stash busting — each section could be a different colour!)

- With or without beads

If knitting shawl in one colour disregard MC and CC change directions.

To knit a version without beads, simply knit the stitch that is indicated PB.

The percentages given are calculated based on the percentage of total stitches in the shawl. This can help guide you regarding how much yarn you need. E.g. if you weigh your yarn at the beginning and then at 10%, it will give you an indication of how much yarn you will need in total.

The pattern is written line-by-line in the checklist format. The eyelet section (rows 79–98 for the medium size and 95–114 in the large size) and the lace border (rows 115–135 in the medium size and 131–151 for the large) are also charted.

From the start of the border section there is no longer a central increase. The marker is removed and increases are only worked at each side of the shawl both on RS and WS as before.

PLACING BEADS

Slip the bead onto the end of your crochet hook (over the hook).

Insert the hook into the stitch loop on the left needle, with the hook facing you.

Gently move the bead down over the hook onto the stitch.

Place the stitch back on the left needle.

Knit the stitch with the bead on it.

See page 83 for more detail.

Size: Medium Yarn: Seven Sisters Arts – Matrika

Medium

ROW	DIRECTIONS	TOTAL STITCHES	% DONE
	Garter Section **MC:** Cast on 5	5	
1	Knit all sts	5	
2	Knit all sts	5	
3	[RS] K1, kfb, k1, kfb, k1	7	
4	[WS] Knit all sts	7	
5	[RS] K1, kfb, k3, kfb, k1	9	
6	[WS] Knit all sts	9	
7	[RS] K3, yo, k1, M1R, PM, k1, M1L, k1, yo, k3	13	
8	[WS] K3, yo, knit to last 3 sts, yo, k3	15	
9	[RS] K3, yo, knit to marker, M1R, SM, k1, M1L, knit to last 3 sts, yo, k3 **(and every RS row in this section)**	19	
10	[WS] K3, yo, knit to last 3 sts, yo, k3 **(and every WS row in this section)**	21	
11	[RS]	25	
12	[WS]	27	
13	[RS]	31	
14	[WS]	33	
15	[RS]	37	
16	[WS]	39	
17	[RS]	43	
18	[WS]	45	
19	[RS]	49	
20	[WS]	51	
21	[RS]	55	
22	[WS]	57	
23	[RS]	61	
24	[WS]	63	
25	[RS]	67	
26	[WS]	69	
27	[RS]	73	
28	[WS]	75	
29	[RS]	79	
30	[WS]	81	
31	[RS]	85	

ROW	DIRECTIONS	TOTAL STITCHES	% DONE
32	[WS]	87	5%
33	[RS]	91	
34	[WS]	93	
35	[RS]	97	
36	[WS]	99	
37	[RS]	103	
38	[WS]	105	
39	[RS]	109	
40	[WS]	111	
41	[RS]	115	
42	[WS]	117	
43	[RS]	121	
44	[WS]	123	
45	[RS]	127	10%
46	[WS]	129	
47	[RS]	133	
48	[WS]	135	
49	[RS]	139	
50	[WS]	141	
51	[RS]	145	
52	[WS]	147	
53	[RS]	151	
54	[WS]	153	
55	[RS]	157	15%
56	[WS]	159	
57	[RS]	163	
58	[WS]	165	
59	[RS]	169	
60	[WS]	171	
61	[RS]	175	
62	[WS]	177	
63	[RS]	181	20%
64	[WS]	183	
65	[RS]	187	
66	[WS]	189	
67	[RS]	193	
68	[WS]	195	

ROW	DIRECTIONS	TOTAL STITCHES	% DONE
69	[RS]	199	
70	[WS]	201	25%
71	[RS]	205	
72	[WS]	207	
73	[RS]	211	
74	[WS]	213	
75	[RS]	217	
76	[WS]	219	30%
77	[RS]	223	
78	[WS]	225	
79	**Eyelet Section** [RS] **CC:** K3, yo, knit to marker, M1R, SM, k1, M1L, knit to last 3 sts, yo, k3 **(and every RS row in this section unless otherwise stated)**	229	
80	[WS] K3, yo, purl to last 3 sts, yo, k3 **(and every WS row In this section)**	231	
81	[RS] K3, yo, k2, *k1, PB, k2tog tbl, yo* to 2 sts before marker, k2, M1R, SM, k1, M1L, k2, *yo, k2tog, PB, k1* to last 5 sts, k2, yo, k3 (54 beads)	235	
82	[WS]	237	35%
83	[RS]	241	
84	[WS]	243	
85	[RS] K3, yo, k3, *yo, k2tog, PB, k1* to 3 sts before marker, yo, k2tog, k1, M1R, SM, k1, M1L, k1, k2tog tbl, yo, *k1, PB, k2tog tbl, yo* to last 6 sts, k3, yo, k3 (56 beads)	247	
86	[WS]	249	
87	[RS]	253	
88	[WS]	255	40%
89	[RS] K3, yo, k2, *k1, PB, k2tog tbl, yo* to 2 sts before marker, k2, M1R, SM, k1, M1L, k2, *yo, k2tog, PB, k1* to last 5 sts, k2, yo, k3 (60 beads)	259	
90	[WS]	261	
91	[RS]	265	
92	[WS]	267	

ROW	DIRECTIONS	TOTAL STITCHES	% DONE
93	[RS] K3, yo, k3, *yo, k2tog, PB, k1* to 3 sts before marker, yo, k2tog, k1, M1R, SM, k1, M1L, k1, k2tog tbl, yo, *k1, PB, k2tog tbl, yo* to last 6 sts, k3, yo, k3 (62 beads)	271	45%
94	[WS]	273	
95	[RS]	277	
96	[WS]	279	
97	[RS] K3, yo, k2, *k1, PB, k2tog tbl, yo* to 2 sts before marker, k2, M1R, SM, k1, M1L, k2, *yo, k2tog, PB, k1* to last 5 sts, k2, yo, k3 (66 beads)	283	
98	[WS]	285	50%
99	**Rib Section** [RS] **MC:** K3, yo, knit to marker, M1R, SM, k1, M1L, knit to last 3 sts, yo, k3	289	
100	[WS] K3, yo, p1, *k3, p1* to 1 st before marker, p1, SM, *p1, k3* to last 4 sts, p1, yo, k3	291	
101	[RS] K3, yo, p1, k1, *p3, k1* to marker, M1R, SM, k1, M1L, *K1, p3* to last 5 sts, k1, p1, yo, k3	295	
102	[WS] K3, yo, k2, p1, *k3, p1* to 2 sts before marker, k1, p1, SM, k1, *p1, k3* to last 6 sts, p1, k2, yo, k3	297	55%
103	[RS] K3, yo, p3, k1, *p3, k1* to 1 st before marker, p1, M1R, SM, k1, M1L, p1, *k1, p3* to last 7 sts, k1, p3, yo, k3	301	
104	[WS] K3, yo, k4, p1, *k3, p1* to 3 sts before marker, k2, p1, SM, k2, *p1, k3* to last 8 sts, p1, k4, yo, k3	303	
105	[RS] K3, yo, p1, k1, *p3, k1* to 2 sts before marker, p2, M1R, SM, k1, M1L, p2, *k1, p3* to last 5 sts, k1, p1, yo, k3	307	
106	[WS] K3, yo, k2, p1, *k3, p1* to 4 sts before marker, k3, p1, SM, k3, *p1, k3* to last 6 sts, p1, k2, yo, k3	309	
107	[RS] K3, yo, p3, k1, *p3, k1* to 3 sts before marker, p3, M1R, SM, k1, M1L, p3, *k1, p3* to last 7 sts, k1, p3, yo, k3	313	60%

Medium

ROW	DIRECTIONS	TOTAL STITCHES	% DONE
108	[WS] K3, yo, k4, p1, *k3, p1* to 5 sts before marker, k4, p1, SM, k4, *p1, k3* to last 8 sts, p1, k4, yo, k3	315	
109	[RS] K3, yo, p1, k1, *p3, k1* to marker, M1R, SM, k1, M1L, *k1, p3* to last 5 sts, k1, p1, yo, k3	319	
110	[WS] K3, yo, k2, p1, *k3, p1* to 2 sts before marker, k1, p1, SM, k1, *p1, k3* to last 6 sts, p1, k2, yo, k3	321	
111	[RS] K3, yo, p3, k1, *p3, k1* to 1 st before marker, p1, M1R, SM, k1, M1L, p1, *k1, p3* to last 7 sts, k1, p3, yo, k3	325	65%
112	[WS] K3, yo, k4, p1, *k3, p1* to 3 sts before marker, k2, p1, SM, k2, *p1, k3* to last 8 sts, p1, k4, yo, k3	327	
113	[RS] K3, yo, p1, k1, *p3, k1* to 2 sts before marker, p2, M1R, SM, k1, M1L, p2, *k1, p3* to last 5 sts, k1, p1, yo, k3	331	
114	[WS] K3, yo, k2, p1, *k3, p1* to 4 sts before marker, k3, p1, remove marker, k3, *p1, k3* to last 6 sts, p1, k2, yo, k3	333	
115	**Border Section** [RS] **CC:** K3, yo, *k1, k2tog, yo, PB, yo, k2tog tbl, k1, p1* to last 10 sts, k1, k2tog, yo, PB, yo, k2tog tbl, k1, yo, k3 *(41 beads)*	335	70%
116	[WS] K3, yo, *k1, p7* to last 4 sts, k1, yo, k3	337	
117	[RS] K3, yo, k1, p1, *k2tog, yo, k3, yo, k2tog tbl, p1* to last 4 sts, k1, yo, k3	339	
118	[WS] K3, yo, p2, *k1, p7* to last 6 sts, k1, p2, yo, k3	341	
119	[RS] K3, yo, k3, p1, *k1, k2tog, yo, PB, yo, k2tog tbl, k1, p1* to last 6 sts, k3, yo, k3 *(41 beads)*	343	75%
120	[WS] K3, yo, p4, *k1, p7* to last 8 sts, k1, p4, yo, k3	345	
121	[RS] K3, yo, k5, p1, *k2tog, yo, k3, yo, k2tog tbl, p1* to last 8 sts, k5, yo, k3	347	
122	[WS] K3, yo, p6, *k1, p7* to last 10 sts, k1, p6, yo, k3	349	
123	[RS] K3, yo, *k1, k2tog, yo, PB, yo, k2tog tbl, k1, p1* to last 10 sts, k1, k2tog, yo, PB, yo, k2tog tbl, k1, yo, k3 *(43 beads)*	351	80%
124	[WS] K3, yo, *k1, p7* to last 4 sts, k1, yo, k3	353	
125	[RS] K3, yo, k1, p1, *k2tog, yo, k3, yo, k2tog tbl, p1* to last 4 sts, k1, yo, k3	355	
126	[WS] K3, yo, p2, *k1, p7* to last 6 sts, k1, p2, yo, k3	357	
127	[RS] K3, yo, k4, *yo, k2, S2KP, k2, yo, k1* to last 6 sts, k3, yo, k3	359	85%
128	[WS] K3, yo, purl to last 3 sts, yo, k3	361	
129	[RS] K3, yo, k6, *k1, yo, k1, S2KP, k1, yo, k2* to last 8 sts, k5, yo, k3	363	
130	[WS] K3, yo, purl to last 3 sts, yo, k3	365	
131	[RS] K3, yo, k8, *k2, yo, S2KP, yo, k3* to last 10 sts, k7, yo, k3	367	90%
132	[WS] K3, yo, purl to last 3 sts, yo, k3	369	
133	[RS] K3, yo, k1, k2tog, *k2, yo, PB, yo, k2, S2KP* to last 11 sts, k2, yo, PB, yo, k2, k2tog tbl, k1, yo, k3 *(45 beads)*	371	
134	[WS] K3, yo, purl to last 3 sts, yo, k3	373	95%
135	[RS] K3, yo, k3, k2tog, *k2, yo, k1, yo, k2, S2KP* to last 13 sts, k2, yo, k1, yo, k2, k2tog tbl, k3, yo, k3	375	
	Cast off: K1, *k1, transfer the 2 sts back to the left needle and k2tog through back loops,* repeat to end		100%

ROW	DIRECTIONS	TOTAL STITCHES	% DONE
	Garter Section **MC:** Cast on 5	5	
1	Knit all sts	5	
2	Knit all sts	5	
3	[RS] K1, kfb, k1, kfb, k1	7	
4	[WS] Knit all sts	7	
5	[RS] K1, kfb, k3, kfb, k1	9	
6	[WS] Knit all sts	9	
7	[RS] K3, yo, k1, M1R, PM, k1, M1L, k1, yo, k3	13	
8	[WS] K3, yo, knit to last 3 sts, yo, k3	15	
9	[RS] K3, yo, knit to marker, M1R, SM, k1, M1L, knit to last 3 sts, yo, k3 **(and every RS row in this section)**	19	
10	[WS] K3, yo, knit to last 3 sts, yo, k3 **(and every WS row In this section)**	21	
11	[RS]	25	
12	[WS]	27	
13	[RS]	31	
14	[WS]	33	
15	[RS]	37	
16	[WS]	39	
17	[RS]	43	
18	[WS]	45	
19	[RS]	49	
20	[WS]	51	
21	[RS]	55	
22	[WS]	57	
23	[RS]	61	
24	[WS]	63	
25	[RS]	67	
26	[WS]	69	
27	[RS]	73	
28	[WS]	75	
29	[RS]	79	
30	[WS]	81	
31	[RS]	85	
32	[WS]	87	
33	[RS]	91	
34	[WS]	93	

ROW	DIRECTIONS	TOTAL STITCHES	% DONE
35	[RS]	97	
36	[WS]	99	5%
37	[RS]	103	
38	[WS]	105	
39	[RS]	109	
40	[WS]	111	
41	[RS]	115	
42	[WS]	117	
43	[RS]	121	
44	[WS]	123	
45	[RS]	127	
46	[WS]	129	
47	[RS]	133	
48	[WS]	135	
49	[RS]	139	
50	[WS]	141	10%
51	[RS]	145	
52	[WS]	147	
53	[RS]	151	
54	[WS]	153	
55	[RS]	157	
56	[WS]	159	
57	[RS]	163	
58	[WS]	165	
59	[RS]	169	
60	[WS]	171	
61	[RS]	175	15%
62	[WS]	177	
63	[RS]	181	
64	[WS]	183	
65	[RS]	187	
66	[WS]	189	
67	[RS]	193	
68	[WS]	195	
69	[RS]	199	
70	[WS]	201	20%
71	[RS]	205	
72	[WS]	207	
73	[RS]	211	

Large

ROW	DIRECTIONS	TOTAL STITCHES	% DONE
74	[WS]	213	
75	[RS]	217	
76	[WS]	219	
77	[RS]	223	
78	[WS]	225	25%
79	[RS]	229	
80	[WS]	231	
81	[RS]	235	
82	[WS]	237	
83	[RS]	241	
84	[WS]	243	
85	[RS]	247	30%
86	[WS]	249	
87	[RS]	253	
88	[WS]	255	
89	[RS]	259	
90	[WS]	261	
91	[RS]	265	
92	[WS]	267	35%
93	[RS]	271	
94	[WS]	273	
95	**Eyelet Section** [RS] **CC:** K3, yo, knit to marker, M1R, SM, k1, M1L, knit to last 3 sts, yo, k3 **(and every RS row in this section unless otherwise stated)**	277	
96	[WS] K3, yo, purl to last 3 sts, yo, k3 **(and every WS row In this section)**	279	
97	[RS] K3, yo, k2, *k1, PB, k2tog tbl, yo* to 2 sts before marker, k2, M1R, SM, k1, M1L, k2, *yo, k2tog, PB, k1* to last 5 sts, k2, yo, k3 *(66 beads)*	283	
98	[WS]	285	40%
99	[RS]	289	
100	[WS]	291	
101	[RS] K3, yo, k3, *yo, k2tog, PB, k1* to 3 sts before marker, yo, k2tog, k1, M1R, SM, k1, M1L, k1, k2tog tbl, yo, *k1, PB, k2tog tbl, yo* to last 6 sts, k3, yo, k3 *(68 beads)*	295	

ROW	DIRECTIONS	TOTAL STITCHES	% DONE
102	[WS]	297	
103	[RS]	301	
104	[WS]	303	45%
105	[RS] K3, yo, k2, *k1, PB, k2tog tbl, yo* to 2 sts before marker, k2, M1R, SM, k1, M1L, k2, *yo, k2tog, PB, k1* to last 5 sts, k2, yo, k3 *(72 beads)*	307	
106	[WS]	309	
107	[RS]	313	
108	[WS]	315	
109	[RS] K3, yo, k3, *yo, k2tog, PB, k1* to 3 sts before marker, yo, k2tog, k1, M1R, SM, k1, M1L, k1, k2tog tbl, yo, *k1, PB, k2tog tbl, yo* to last 6 sts, k3, yo, k3 *(74 beads)*	319	50%
110	[WS]	321	
111	[RS]	325	
112	[WS]	327	
113	[RS] K3, yo, k2, *k1, PB, k2tog tbl, yo* to 2 sts before marker, k2, M1R, SM, k1, M1L, k2, *yo, k2tog, PB, k1* to last 5 sts, k2, yo, k3 *(78 beads)*	331	
114	[WS]	333	55%
115	**Rib Section** [RS] **MC:** K3, yo, knit to marker, M1R, SM, k1, M1L, knit to last 3 sts, yo, k3	337	
116	[WS] K3, yo, p1, *k3, p1* to 1 st before marker, p1, SM, *p1, k3* to last 4 sts, p1, yo, k3	339	
117	[RS] K3, yo, p1, k1, *p3, k1* to marker, M1R, SM, k1, M1L, *K1, p3* to last 5 sts, k1, p1, yo, k3	343	
118	[WS] K3, yo, k2, p1, *k3, p1* to 2 sts before marker, k1, p1, SM, k1, *p1, k3* to last 6 sts, p1, k2, yo, k3	345	
119	[RS] K3, yo, p3, k1, *p3, k1* to 1 st before marker, p1, M1R, SM, k1, M1L, p1, *k1, p3* to last 7 sts, k1, p3, yo, k3	349	60%
120	[WS] K3, yo, k4, p1, *k3, p1* to 3 sts before marker, k2, p1, SM, k2, *p1, k3* to last 8 sts, p1, k4, yo, k3	351	

ROW	DIRECTIONS	TOTAL STITCHES	% DONE
121	[RS] K3, yo, p1, k1, *p3, k1* to 2 sts before marker, p2, M1R, SM, k1, M1L, p2, *k1, p3* to last 5 sts, k1, p1, yo, k3	355	
122	[WS] K3, yo, k2, p1, *k3, p1* to 4 sts before marker, k3, p1, SM, k3, *p1, k3* to last 6 sts, p1, k2, yo, k3	357	
123	[RS] K3, yo, p3, k1, *p3, k1* to 3 sts before marker, p3, M1R, SM, k1, M1L, p3, *k1, p3* to last 7 sts, k1, p3, yo, k3	361	
124	[WS] K3, yo, k4, p1, *k3, p1* to 5 sts before marker, k4, p1, SM, k4, *p1, k3* to last 8 sts, p1, k4, yo, k3	363	65%
125	[RS] K3, yo, p1, k1, *p3, k1* to marker, M1R, SM, k1, M1L, *k1, p3* to last 5 sts, k1, p1, yo, k3	367	
126	[WS] K3, yo, k2, p1, *k3, p1* to 2 sts before marker, k1, p1, SM, k1, *p1, k3* to last 6 sts, p1, k2, yo, k3	369	
127	[RS] K3, yo, p3, k1, *p3, k1* to 1 st before marker, p1, M1R, SM, k1, M1L, p1, *k1, p3* to last 7 sts, k1, p3, yo, k3	373	
128	[WS] K3, yo, k4, p1, *k3, p1* to 3 sts before marker, k2, p1, SM, k2, *p1, k3* to last 8 sts, p1, k4, yo, k3	375	
129	[RS] K3, yo, p1, k1, *p3, k1* to 2 sts before marker, p2, M1R, SM, k1, M1L, p2, *k1, p3* to last 5 sts, k1, p1, yo, k3	379	70%
130	[WS] K3, yo, k2, p1, *k3, p1* to 4 sts before marker, k3, p1, remove marker, k3, *p1, k3* to last 6 sts, p1, k2, yo, k3	381	
131	**Border Section** [RS] CC: K3, yo, *k1, k2tog, yo, PB, yo, k2tog tbl, k1, p1* to last 10 sts, k1, k2tog, yo, PB, yo, k2tog tbl, k1, yo, k3 (47 beads)	383	
132	[WS] K3, yo, *k1, p7* to last 4 sts, k1, yo, k3	385	
133	[RS] K3, yo, k1, p1, *k2tog, yo, k3, yo, k2tog tbl, p1* to last 4 sts, k1, yo, k3	387	75%
134	[WS] K3, yo, p2, *k1, p7* to last 6 sts, k1, p2, yo, k3	389	

ROW	DIRECTIONS	TOTAL STITCHES	% DONE
135	[RS] K3, yo, k3, p1, *k1, k2tog, yo, PB, yo, k2tog tbl, k1, p1* to last 6 sts, k3, yo, k3 (47 beads)	391	
136	[WS] K3, yo, p4, *k1, p7* to last 8 sts, k1, p4, yo, k3	393	
137	[RS] K3, yo, k5, p1, *k2tog, yo, k3, yo, k2tog tbl, p1* to last 8 sts, k5, yo, k3	395	80%
138	[WS] K3, yo, p6, *k1, p7* to last 10 sts, k1, p6, yo, k3	397	
139	[RS] K3, yo, *k1, k2tog, yo, PB, yo, k2tog tbl, k1, p1* to last 10 sts, k1, k2tog, yo, PB, yo, k2tog tbl, k1, yo, k3 (49 beads)	399	
140	[WS] K3, yo, *k1, p7* to last 4 sts, k1, yo, k3	401	
141	[RS] K3, yo, k1, p1, *k2tog, yo, k3, yo, k2tog tbl, p1* to last 4 sts, k1, yo, k3	403	
142	[WS] K3, yo, p2, *k1, p7* to last 6 sts, k1, p2, yo, k3	405	85%
143	[RS] K3, yo, k4, *yo, k2, S2KP, k2, yo, k1* to last 6 sts, k3, yo, k3	407	
144	[WS] K3, yo, purl to last 3 sts, yo, k3	409	
145	[RS] K3, yo, k6, *k1, yo, k1, S2KP, k1, yo, k2* to last 8 sts, k5, yo, k3	411	
146	[WS] K3, yo, purl to last 3 sts, yo, k3	413	90%
147	[RS] K3, yo, k8, *k2, yo, S2KP, yo, k3* to last 10 sts, k7, yo, k3	415	
148	[WS] K3, yo, purl to last 3 sts, yo, k3	417	
149	[RS] K3, yo, k1, k2tog, *k2, yo, PB, yo, k2, S2KP* to last 11 sts, k2, yo, PB, yo, k2, k2tog tbl, k1, yo, k3 (51 beads)	419	
150	[WS] K3, yo, purl to last 3 sts, yo, k3	421	95%
151	[RS] K3, yo, k3, k2tog, *k2, yo, k1, yo, k2, S2KP* to last 13 sts, k2, yo, k1, yo, k2, k2tog tbl, k3, yo, k3	423	
	Cast off: K1, *k1, transfer the 2 sts back to the left needle and k2tog through back loops,* repeat to end		100%

Charts

Charts are read from bottom to top. They are read right to left on right side rows, and left to right on wrong side rows.

For Charts B–D, row numbers corresponding to the written directions are displayed to the right of each chart.

The area in the bold box indicates a repeat.

CHART KEY

☐	knit on RS, purl on WS
☐•	purl on RS, knit on WS
☐O	yo
☐/	k2tog
☐\	k2tog tbl
☐B	place bead
☐⋀	S2KP
☐R	make 1 right
☐L	make 1 left
▦	no stitch
☐	pattern repeat

Size: Large Yarn: Madelinetosh Tosh Merino Light

EYELET SECTION

This section corresponds to:
Medium Size rows 79–98
Large Size rows 95–114

CHART A

Work rows 1–10 once
Then work rows 3–10 once more
Then work rows 3–4 once more

BORDER SECTION

This section corresponds to:
Medium Size rows 115–135
Large Size rows 131–151

CHART D

																									MED	LGE
		O			\		O		O		Λ		O		O			/			O				135	151
	•	•	•	O																O	•	•	•			
			O	\		O	B	O		Λ		O	B	O		/		O						133	149

CHART C

																							MED	LGE
•	•	•	O													O	•	•	•				131	147
		O					O	Λ	O			O											129	145
	•	•	•	O		O		Λ		O			O	•	•	•							127	143
			O		O		Λ		O		O		•	•	•								125	141
				O	•	\	O			O	/	•	O										

CHART B

																									MED	LGE
•	•	•	O	•				•					•					•	O	•	•	•				
		O		\	O	B	O	/	•		\	O	B	O	/	•	\	O	B	O	/	O			123	139
	•	•	•	O	•				•					•		O	•	•	•						121	137
			O	•	\	O		O	/	•				O											119	135
	•	•	•	O	•		\	O	B	O	/	•		O										117	133
				O	•	\	O		O	/	•	O												115	131

FINISHING

Weave in ends.

BLOCKING

For detailed blocking instructions see page 82.

ASANA
Shawl

A gentle crescent shawl with flowing lace and garter sections, Asana is a lovely special occasion shawl, whether you're preparing for one magical day or making an ordinary day magical through a bit of mindfulness.

Optional beads add a flicker of light to its soft textures and quiet curves. Designed for lace or fingering weight yarn, it is delicate and light enough to wear even in the warmer months.

In yoga, Asana means "a position that is firm, but relaxed." This attitude should be familiar to anyone who has ever learned to knit, or tried a new technique just outside your comfort zone. Gritting your teeth and clenching your hands around your needles never helps. This shawl is a higher level of difficulty than the previous Shawl Society patterns: the lace is a bit more challenging and there are four rows where you are knitting lace rows on the wrong side. The actual stitches aren't difficult, but you need to be in meditation mode (not multitasking mode). Concentration, relaxation and focus will get you through to the graceful result you want.

Left: Size Medium Yarn: The Uncommon Thread Tough Sock
Above: Size Large Yarn: Eden Cottage Yarn Theseus Lace

Size: Large Yarn: Eden Cottage Yarn Theseus Lace

SPECIFICATIONS

SIZE

Medium, Large

FINISHED MEASUREMENTS

Medium

Approximately 183cm (72") diameter across straight top edge
46cm (18") neck to bottom edge

Large

Approximately 213cm (84") diameter across straight top edge
46cm (18") neck to bottom edge

YARN

Medium

The Uncommon Thread Tough Sock [80% Superwash Bluefaced Leicester wool, 20% Nylon, 365m/400yds per 100g skein], 2 x 100g skeins, Colourway: Smudge
OR
200g of fingering or sock weight yarn totalling approximately 730m/800yds

Large

Eden Cottage Yarn Theseus Lace [75% Merino wool, 25% Silk, 800m/872yds per 100g skein], 1 x 100g skein, Colourway: Oak
OR
80g of lace weight yarn totalling approximately 640m/698yds

NEEDLES

Medium

4mm (US 6), 80/100cm (32/40") long circular needles (or size to obtain gauge)

Large

3.75mm (US 5), 80/100cm (32/40") long circular needles (or size to obtain gauge)

NOTIONS

Tapestry needle
Removable marker or safety pin
If using beads (optional)
US Steel Size 12/1.0mm Crochet hook (or hook small enough to fit through holes in beads)

Medium

Approx. 375 beads / 30g size 6 seed beads (beads used in sample are Miyuki beads)

Large

Approx. 440 beads / 35g size 6 seed beads

GAUGE

Medium

19 sts/32 rows = 10cm (4") in garter stitch after blocking

Large

22 sts/38 rows = 10cm (4") in garter stitch after blocking

ASANA NOTES

This shawl is knit from the top down.

The shawl is crescent in shape and increases are made at the edges. Two stitches are increased each RS edge (4 sts increased each RS row in total) and one stitch is increased each WS edge (2 sts increased each WS row in total).

The percentages given are calculated based on the percentage of total stitches in the shawl. This can help guide you regarding how much yarn you need. E.g. if you weigh your yarn at the beginning and then at 10%, it will give you an indication of how much yarn you will need in total.

Pay special attention to the border stitches throughout the shawl. The KYOK stitch is tricky to fix after you have passed that row so pay careful attention to whether you are on a RS row working a KYOK or a WS row working a YO.

The PB abbreviation counts as one stitch. You place the bead then knit the same stitch. To knit a version without beads, simply knit the stitch that is indicated PB.

After a few rows place a pin or stitch marker on the right side so you can see at a glance which side is which.

The pattern is written in the percentage checklist style; the lace section is also charted for those who prefer it.

The heavy border in the following instructions indicates the same lace pattern repeated three times.

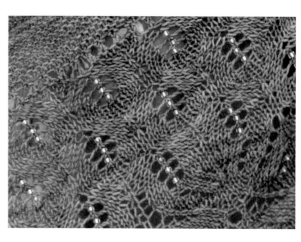

PLACING BEADS

Slip the bead onto the end of your crochet hook (over the hook).

Insert the hook into the stitch loop on the left needle, with the hook facing you.

Gently move the bead down over the hook onto the stitch.

Place the stitch back on the left needle.

Knit the stitch with the bead on it.

Size: Medium Yarn: The Uncommon Thread Tough Sock

Medium

ROW	DIRECTIONS	TOTAL STITCHES	% DONE
	Garter Section Cast on 7 sts using long tail or knitted method		
1	[WS] Knit all sts	7	
2	[RS] Knit all sts	7	
3	[WS] Knit all sts	7	
4	[RS] K2, kfb, k1, kfb, k2	9	
5	[WS] K2, [yo, k1] 6 times, k1	15	
6	[RS] K3, KYOK, k7, KYOK, k3	19	
7	[WS] K3, yo, knit to last 3 sts, yo, k3 **(and every WS row In this section)**	21	
8	[RS] K3, KYOK, knit to last 4 sts, KYOK, k3 **(and all following RS rows unless stated otherwise)**	25	
9	[WS]	27	
10	[RS] Place removable marker or safety pin to mark right side of work	31	
11	[WS]	33	
12	[RS]	37	
13	[WS]	39	
14	[RS]	43	
15	[WS]	45	
16	[RS]	49	
17	[WS]	51	
18	[RS]	55	
19	[WS]	57	
20	[RS]	61	
21	[WS]	63	
22	[RS]	67	
23	[WS]	69	
24	[RS]	73	
25	[WS]	75	
26	[RS]	79	
27	[WS]	81	
28	[RS]	85	
29	[WS]	87	
30	[RS]	91	
31	[WS]	93	
32	[RS]	97	5%
33	[WS]	99	
34	[RS]	103	

ROW	DIRECTIONS	TOTAL STITCHES	% DONE
35	[WS]	105	
36	[RS]	109	
37	[WS]	111	
38	[RS]	115	
39	[WS]	117	
40	[RS]	121	
41	[WS]	123	
42	[RS]	127	
43	[WS]	129	
44	[RS]	133	
45	[WS]	135	
46	[RS]	139	10%
47	[WS]	141	
48	[RS]	145	
49	[WS]	147	
50	[RS]	151	
51	[WS]	153	
52	[RS]	157	
53	[WS]	159	
54	[RS]	163	
55	[WS]	165	
56	[RS]	169	15%
57	[WS]	171	
58	[RS]	175	
59	[WS]	177	
60	[RS]	181	
61	[WS]	183	
62	[RS]	187	
63	[WS]	189	
64	[RS]	193	
65	[WS]	195	20%
66	[RS]	199	
67	[WS]	201	
68	[RS]	205	
69	[WS]	207	
70	[RS]	211	
71	[WS]	213	
72	[RS]	217	25%
73	[WS]	219	
74	[RS]	223	
75	[WS]	225	

ROW	DIRECTIONS	TOTAL STITCHES	% DONE
76	[RS]	229	
77	[WS]	231	
78	[RS]	235	
79	[WS]	237	30%
80	[RS]	241	
81	[WS]	243	
82	[RS] K3, KYOK, *k2tog, yo* knit to last 5 sts, k1, KYOK, k3	247	
83	[WS]	249	
84	**Lace Section** [RS] K3, KYOK, k1, *k1, k2tog, k1, KYOK, k1, ssk, k2* repeat to last 4 sts, KYOK, k3	253	
85	[WS] K3, yo, purl to last 3 sts, yo, k3 **(and every WS row In this section)**	255	
86	[RS] K3, KYOK, k4, *k2tog, k2, yo, PB, yo, k2, ssk, k1* repeat to last 7 sts, k3, KYOK, k3 (24 beads)	259	35%
87	[WS]	261	
88	[RS] K3, KYOK, k6, k2tog, *k3, yo, PB, yo, k3, S2KP* repeat to last 19 sts, k3, yo, PB, yo, k3, ssk, k6, KYOK, k3 (24 beads)	265	
89	[WS]	267	
90	[RS] K3, KYOK, k9, k2tog, *k3, yo, PB, yo, k3, S2KP* repeat to last 22 sts, k3, yo, PB, yo, k3, ssk, k9, KYOK, k3 (24 beads)	271	
91	[WS]	273	
92	[RS]	277	40%
93	[WS]	279	
94	[RS] K3, KYOK, k1, *k1, k2tog, k1, KYOK, k1, ssk, k2* repeat to last 4 sts, KYOK, k3	283	
95	[WS]	285	
96	[RS] K3, KYOK, k4, *k2tog, k2, yo, PB, yo, k2, ssk, k1* repeat to last 7 sts, k3, KYOK, k3 (27 beads)	289	
97	[WS]	291	45%
98	[RS] K3, KYOK, k6, k2tog, *k3, yo, PB, yo, k3, S2KP* repeat to last 19 sts, k3, yo, PB, yo, k3, ssk, k6, KYOK, k3 (27 beads)	295	
99	[WS]	297	

ROW	DIRECTIONS	TOTAL STITCHES	% DONE
100	[RS] K3, KYOK, k9, k2tog, *k3, yo, PB, yo, k3, S2KP* repeat to last 22 sts, k3, yo, PB, yo, k3, ssk, k9, KYOK, k3 (27 beads)	301	
101	[WS]	303	
102	[RS]	307	50%
103	[WS]	309	
104	[RS] K3, KYOK, k1, *k1, k2tog, k1, KYOK, k1, ssk, k2* repeat to last 4 sts, KYOK, k3	313	
105	[WS]	315	
106	[RS] K3, KYOK, k4, *k2tog, k2, yo, PB, yo, k2, ssk, k1* repeat to last 7 sts, k3, KYOK, k3 (30 beads)	319	
107	[WS]	321	55%
108	[RS] K3, KYOK, k6, k2tog, *k3, yo, PB, yo, k3, S2KP* repeat to last 19 sts, k3, yo, PB, yo, k3, ssk, k6, KYOK, k3 (30 beads)	325	
109	[WS]	327	
110	[RS] K3, KYOK, k9, k2tog, *k3, yo, PB, yo, k3, S2KP* repeat to last 22 sts, k3, yo, PB, yo, k3, ssk, k9, KYOK, k3 (30 beads)	331	
111	[WS]	333	
112	[RS]	337	60%
113	[WS]	339	
114	[RS] K3, KYOK, k3, k2tog, yo, k1, *yo, ssk, k2, yo, k2, ssk, k3, k2tog, k2, yo, k2, k2tog, yo, k1* repeat to last 9 sts, yo, ssk, k3, KYOK, k3	343	
115	[WS]	345	
116	[RS] K3, KYOK, k5, k2tog, yo, k2, *k1, yo, ssk, k2, yo, k2, ssk, k1, k2tog, k2, yo, k2, k2tog, yo, k2* repeat to last 12 sts, k1, yo, ssk, k5, KYOK, k3	349	
117	[WS]	351	65%
118	[RS] K3, KYOK, k7, k2tog, yo, k3, *k2, yo, ssk, k2, yo, k2, S2KP, k2, yo, k2, k2tog, yo, k3* repeat to last 15 sts, k2, yo, ssk, k7, KYOK, k3	355	
119	[WS]	357	
120	[RS] K3, KYOK, k5, *k4, k2tog, yo, k7, yo, ssk, k5* repeat to last 8 sts, k4, KYOK, k3	361	

Medium

ROW	DIRECTIONS	TOTAL STITCHES	% DONE
121	[WS] K3, yo, p7, *p4, p2tog tbl, p4, yo, p1, yo, p4, p2tog, p3* repeat to last 11 sts, p8, yo, k3	363	
122	[RS] K3, KYOK, k8, *k2, k2tog, k4, yo, k3, yo, k4, ssk, k3* repeat to last 11 sts, k7, KYOK, K3	367	
123	[WS] K3, yo, p10, *p2, p2tog tbl, p4, yo, p5, yo, p4, p2tog, p1* repeat to last 14 sts, p11, yo, k3	369	70%
124	[RS] K3, KYOK, k11, *k2tog, k4, yo, k7, yo, k4, ssk, k1* repeat to last 14 sts, k10, KYOK, K3	373	
125	[WS]	375	
126	[RS] K3, KYOK, k4, *k1, PB, k5, k2tog, yo, k1, yo, ssk, k5, PB, k2* repeat to last 7 sts, k3, KYOK, k3 *(36 beads)*	379	
127	[WS]	381	75%
128	[RS] K3, KYOK, k7, *k2, PB, k3, k2tog, yo, k3, yo, ssk, k3, PB, k3* repeat to last 10 sts, k6, KYOK, k3 *(36 beads)*	385	
129	[WS]	387	
130	[RS] K3, KYOK, k2, yo, ssk, k6, *k5, k2tog, yo, k5, yo, ssk, k6* repeat to last 13 sts, k5, k2tog, yo, k2, KYOK, k3	391	
131	[WS]	393	80%
132	[RS] K3, KYOK, k3, *k3, yo, ssk, k9, k2tog, yo, k4* repeat to last 6 sts, k2, KYOK, k3	397	
133	[WS] K3, yo, p5, *p1, yo, p4, p2tog, p7, p2tog tbl, p4, yo* repeat to last 9 sts, p6, yo, k3	399	
134	[RS] K3, KYOK, k6, *k1, yo, k4, ssk, k5, k2tog, k4, yo, k2* repeat to last 9sts, k5, KYOK, k3	403	
135	[WS] K3, yo, p8, *p3, yo, p4, p2tog, p3, p2tog tbl, p4, yo, p2* repeat to last 12 sts, p9, yo, k3	405	85%
136	[RS] K3, KYOK, k8, PB, *k3, yo, k4, ssk, k1, k2tog, k4, yo, k3, PB* repeat to last 12 sts, k8, KYOK, k3 *(20 beads)*	409	
137	[WS]	411	
138	[RS] K3, KYOK, k10, yo, S2KP, *yo, k7, yo, S2KP* repeat to last 14 sts, yo, k10, KYOK, k3	415	

ROW	DIRECTIONS	TOTAL STITCHES	% DONE
139	[WS]	417	90%
140	[RS] K3, KYOK, k12, yo, k1, S2KP, *k1, yo, k5, yo, k1, S2KP* repeat to last 17 sts, k1, yo, k12, KYOK, k3	421	
141	[WS]	423	
142	[RS] K3, KYOK, k14, yo, k2, S2KP, *k2, yo, k3, yo, k2, S2KP* repeat to last 20 sts, k2, yo, k14, KYOK, k3	427	
143	[WS]	429	95%
144	[RS] K3, KYOK, k15, PB, yo, k3, S2KP, *k3, yo, PB, yo, k3, S2KP* repeat to last 23 sts, k3, yo, PB, k15, KYOK, k3	433	
	Cast off: k1, *k1, transfer the 2 sts back to the left hand needle and k2tog through back loops* repeat to end		100%

ROW	DIRECTIONS	TOTAL STITCHES	% DONE
	Garter Section Cast on 7 using long tail or knitted method		
1	[WS] Knit all sts	7	
2	[RS] Knit all sts	7	
3	[WS] Knit all sts	7	
4	[RS] K2, kfb, k1, kfb, k2	9	
5	[WS] K2, [yo, k1] 6 times, k1	15	
6	[RS] K3, KYOK, k7, KYOK, k3	19	
7	[WS] K3, yo, knit to last 3 sts, yo, k3 **(and every WS row in this section)**	21	
8	[RS] K3, KYOK, knit to last 4 sts, kyok, k3 **(and all following RS rows unless stated otherwise)**	25	
9	[WS]	27	
10	[RS] Place removable marker or safety pin to mark right side of work	31	
11	[WS]	33	
12	[RS]	37	
13	[WS]	39	
14	[RS]	43	
15	[WS]	45	
16	[RS]	49	
17	[WS]	51	
18	[RS]	55	
19	[WS]	57	
20	[RS]	61	
21	[WS]	63	
22	[RS]	67	
23	[WS]	69	
24	[RS]	73	
25	[WS]	75	
26	[RS]	79	
27	[WS]	81	
28	[RS]	85	
29	[WS]	87	
30	[RS]	91	
31	[WS]	93	
32	[RS]	97	
33	[WS]	99	

ROW	DIRECTIONS	TOTAL STITCHES	% DONE
34	[RS]	103	
35	[WS]	105	
36	[RS]	109	
37	[WS]	111	5%
38	[RS]	115	
39	[WS]	117	
40	[RS]	121	
41	[WS]	123	
42	[RS]	127	
43	[WS]	129	
44	[RS]	133	
45	[WS]	135	
46	[RS]	139	
47	[WS]	141	
48	[RS]	145	
49	[WS]	147	
50	[RS]	151	
51	[WS]	153	
52	[RS]	157	10%
53	[WS]	159	
54	[RS]	163	
55	[WS]	165	
56	[RS]	169	
57	[WS]	171	
58	[RS]	175	
59	[WS]	177	
60	[RS]	181	
61	[WS]	183	
62	[RS]	187	
63	[WS]	189	
64	[RS]	193	15%
65	[WS]	195	
66	[RS]	199	
67	[WS]	201	
68	[RS]	205	
69	[WS]	207	
70	[RS]	211	
71	[WS]	213	
72	[RS]	217	
73	[WS]	219	

Large

ROW	DIRECTIONS	TOTAL STITCHES	% DONE
74	[RS]	223	20%
75	[WS]	225	
76	[RS]	229	
77	[WS]	231	
78	[RS]	235	
79	[WS]	237	
80	[RS]	241	
81	[WS]	243	
82	[RS]	247	
83	[WS]	249	25%
84	[RS]	253	
85	[WS]	255	
86	[RS]	259	
87	[WS]	261	
88	[RS]	265	
89	[WS]	267	
90	[RS]	271	
91	[WS]	273	
92	[RS]	277	30%
93	[WS]	279	
94	[RS]	283	
95	[WS]	285	
96	[RS]	289	
97	[WS]	291	
98	[RS]	295	35%
99	[WS]	297	
100	[RS]	301	
101	[WS]	303	
102	[RS] K3, KYOK, *k2tog, yo* knit to last 5 sts, k1, KYOK, k3	307	
103	[WS]	309	
104	**Lace Section** [RS] K3, KYOK, k1, *k1, k2tog, k1, KYOK, k1, ssk, k2* repeat to last 4 sts, KYOK, k3	313	
105	[WS] K3, yo, purl to last 3 sts, yo, k3 **(and every WS row In this section)**	315	40%
106	[RS] K3, KYOK, k4, *k2tog, k2, yo, PB, yo, k2, ssk, k1* repeat to last 7 sts, k3, KYOK, k3 (30 beads)	319	
107	[WS]	321	

ROW	DIRECTIONS	TOTAL STITCHES	% DONE
108	[RS] K3, KYOK, k6, k2tog, *k3, yo, PB, yo, k3, S2KP* repeat to last 19 sts, k3, yo, PB, yo, k3, ssk, k6, KYOK, k3 (30 beads)	325	
109	[WS]	327	
110	[RS] K3, KYOK, k9, k2tog, *k3, yo, PB, yo, k3, S2KP* repeat to last 22 sts, k3, yo, PB, yo, k3, ssk, k9, KYOK, k3 (30 beads)	331	
111	[WS]	333	
112	[RS]	337	45%
113	[WS]	339	
114	[RS] K3, KYOK, k1, *k1, k2tog, k1, KYOK, k1, ssk, k2* repeat to last 4 sts, KYOK, k3	343	
115	[WS]	345	
116	[RS] K3, KYOK, k4, *k2tog, k2, yo, PB, yo, k2, ssk, k1* repeat to last 7 sts, k3, KYOK, k3 33 beads)	349	
117	[WS]	351	
118	[RS] K3, KYOK, k6, k2tog, *k3, yo, PB, yo, k3, S2KP* repeat to last 19 sts, k3, yo, PB, yo, k3, ssk, k6, KYOK, k3 (33 beads)	355	50%
119	[WS]	357	
120	[RS] K3, KYOK, k9, k2tog, *k3, yo, PB, yo, k3, S2KP* repeat to last 22 sts, k3, yo, PB, yo, k3, ssk, k9, KYOK, k3 (33 beads)	361	
121	[WS]	363	
122	[RS]	367	
123	[WS]	369	55%
124	[RS] K3, KYOK, k1, *k1, k2tog, k1, KYOK, k1, ssk, k2* repeat to last 4 sts, KYOK, k3	373	
125	[WS]	375	
126	[RS] K3, KYOK, k4, *k2tog, k2, yo, PB, yo, k2, ssk, k1* repeat to last 7 sts, k3, KYOK, k3 (36 beads)	379	
127	[WS]	381	
128	[RS] K3, KYOK, k6, k2tog, *k3, yo, PB, yo, k3, S2KP* repeat to last 19 sts, k3, yo, PB, yo, k3, ssk, k6, KYOK, k3 (36 beads)	385	
129	[WS]	387	60%

ROW	DIRECTIONS	TOTAL STITCHES	% DONE
130	[RS] K3, KYOK, k9, k2tog, *k3, yo, PB, yo, k3, S2KP* repeat to last 22 sts, k3, yo, PB, yo, k3, ssk, k9, KYOK, k3 *(36 beads)*	391	
131	[WS]	393	
132	[RS]	397	
133	[WS]	399	
134	[RS] K3, KYOK, k3, k2tog, yo, k1, *yo, ssk, k2, yo, k2, ssk, k3, k2tog, k2, yo, k2, k2tog, yo, k1* repeat to last 9 sts, yo, ssk, k3, KYOK, k3	403	65%
135	[WS]	405	
136	[RS] K3, KYOK, k5, k2tog, yo, k2, *k1, yo, ssk, k2, yo, k2, ssk, k1, k2tog, k2, yo, k2, k2tog, yo, k2* repeat to last 12 sts, k1, yo, ssk, k5, KYOK, k3	409	
137	[WS]	411	
138	[RS] K3, KYOK, k7, k2tog, yo, k3, *k2, yo, ssk, k2, yo, k2, S2KP, k2, yo, k2, k2tog, yo, k3* repeat to last 15 sts, k2, yo, ssk, k7, KYOK, k3	415	
139	[WS]	417	70%
140	[RS] K3, KYOK, k5, *k4, k2tog, yo, k7, yo, ssk, k5* repeat to last 8 sts, k4, KYOK, k3	421	
141	[WS] K3, yo, p7, *p4, p2tog tbl, p4, yo, p1, yo, p4, p2tog, p3* repeat to last 11 sts, p8, yo, k3	423	
142	[RS] K3, KYOK, k8, *k2, k2tog, k4, yo, k3, yo, k4, ssk, k3* repeat to last 11 sts, k7, KYOK, k3	427	
143	[WS] K3, yo, p10, *p2, p2tog tbl, p4, yo, p5, yo, p4, p2tog, p1* repeat to last 14 sts, p11, yo, k3	429	
144	[RS] K3, KYOK, k11, *k2tog, k4, yo, k7, yo, k4, ssk, k1* repeat to last 14 sts, k10, KYOK, k3	433	75%
145	[WS]	435	
146	[RS] K3, KYOK, k4, *k1, PB, k5, k2tog, yo, k1, yo, ssk, k5, PB, k2* repeat to last 7 sts, k3, KYOK, k3 *(42 beads)*	439	
147	[WS]	441	

ROW	DIRECTIONS	TOTAL STITCHES	% DONE
148	[RS] K3, KYOK, k7, *k2, PB, k3, k2tog, yo, k3, yo, ssk, k3, PB, k3* repeat to last 10 sts, k6, KYOK, k3 *(42 beads)*	445	
149	[WS]	447	80%
150	[RS] K3, KYOK, k2, yo, ssk, k6, *k5, k2tog, yo, k5, yo, ssk, k6* repeat to last 13 sts, k5, k2tog, yo, k2, KYOK, k3	451	
151	[WS]	453	
152	[RS] K3, KYOK, k3, *k3, yo, ssk, k9, k2tog, yo, k4* repeat to last 6 sts, k2, KYOK, k3	457	
153	[WS] K3, yo, p5, *p1, yo, p4, p2tog, p7, p2tog tbl, p4, yo* repeat to last 9 sts, p6, yo, k3	459	85%
154	[RS] K3, KYOK, k6, *k1, yo, k4, ssk, k5, k2tog, k4, yo, k2* repeat to last 9 sts, k5, KYOK, k3	463	
155	[WS] K3, yo, p8, *p3, yo, p4, p2tog, p3, p2tog tbl, p4, yo, p2* repeat to last 12 sts, p9, yo, k3	465	
156	[RS] K3, KYOK, k8, PB, *k3, yo, k4, ssk, k1, k2tog, k4, yo, k3, PB* repeat to last 12 sts, k8, KYOK, k3 *(23 beads)*	469	
157	[WS]	471	
158	[RS] K3, KYOK, k10, yo, S2KP, *yo, k7, yo, S2KP* repeat to last 14 sts, yo, k10, KYOK, k3	475	90%
159	[WS]	477	
160	[RS] K3, KYOK, k12, yo, k1, S2KP, *k1, yo, k5, yo, k1, S2KP* repeat to last 17 sts, k1, yo, k12, KYOK, k3	481	
161	[WS]	483	
162	[RS] K3, KYOK, k14, yo, k2, S2KP, *k2, yo, k3, yo, k2, S2KP* repeat to last 20 sts, k2, yo, k14, KYOK, k3	487	95%
163	[WS]	489	
164	[RS] K3, KYOK, k15, PB, yo, k3, S2KP, *k3, yo, PB, yo, k3, S2KP* repeat to last 23 sts, k3, yo, PB, k15, KYOK, k3	493	
	Cast off: K1, *k1, transfer the 2 sts back to the left hand needle and k2tog through back loops,* repeat to end		100%

Charts

Charts are read from bottom to top. They are read right to left on right side rows, and left to right on wrong side rows.

Row numbers corresponding to the written directions are displayed to the right of each chart.

Chart A is repeated 3 times, as indicated below.

Begin with Chart A and work through the charts in alphabetical order.

CHART KEY

☐	knit on right side, purl on wrong side
•	purl on right side, knit on wrong side
O	yo
/	on right side k2tog, p2tog on wrong side
\	on right side ssk, p2tog tbl on wrong side
V	KYOK
Λ	S2KP
B	place bead
▨	no stitch
☐	pattern repeat

Size Medium Yarn The Uncommon Thread Tough Sock

CHART A

MED LGE

		MED	LGE
		92	112
		90	110
		88	108
		86	106
		84	104

Medium Size

Repeat chart A twice more for rows 94–103 and 104–113 before going on to chart B.

Large Size

Repeat chart A twice more for rows 114–123 and 124–133 before going on to chart B.

CHART F

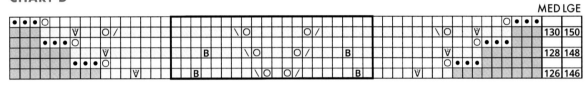

CHART E

CHART D

CHART C

CHART B

FINISHING

Weave in ends.

BLOCKING

For detailed blocking instructions see page 82.

QUILL

Shawl

The design for Quill draws from older, more patient ways of making and doing. This elongated, triangular shawl features stripes like the lines of a letter on a parchment page and a lace border inspired by feathers. Dream dictionaries say that to dream of writing with a quill pen "symbolizes the way you view your creative process – slow, methodical, beautiful, and not very technological."

For me, that lines up beautifully with the way I approach my knitting, and the way I imagine the Quill shawl in the world.

Quill is a generously sized shawl with an engaging mix of colour and texture. It makes for relaxing knitting, and the yarn selected adds another layer of old-fashioned comfort. Tamar DK yarn from Blacker Yarns is a soft, squishy DK weight with rustic charm and a sophisticated colour palette. It is made from historic Wensleydale, Teeswater, Cotswold and Black Leicester Longwool, all British heritage breeds chosen for their long, wavy, lustre fleece. A generous helping of local Cornish mule lambs' fleece gives this yarn extra bounce and give.

Even though the knitting community today is largely bound together by the modern magic of the Internet, the objects we make with our hands are a throwback to a graceful past. Knitting Quill is a beautiful way to slow down at the end of a busy day, giving yourself over to an uncomplicated creative practice and a quieter way of being in the world.

Yarn: Blacker Yarn Tamar DK

SPECIFICATIONS

SIZE
One Size

FINISHED MEASUREMENTS
172cm (68") across top edge
76cm (30") neck to bottom edge

YARN
Blacker Yarns Tamar DK
[30% Cornish mule, 18% Wensleydale, 18% Teeswater, 17% Cotswold, 17% Leicester Longwool, 220m/241yds per 100g skein], 3 x 100g skeins,

Colour A: Gwindra
Colour B: Ottery
Colour C: Tiddy Brook

OR

Approximately 3 x 100g skeins of DK weight yarn totalling approximately 660m/723 yds

NEEDLES
5mm (US 8), 100cm (40) long circular needles (or size to obtain gauge)

NOTIONS
Tapestry needle
1 Stitch marker

GAUGE
14 sts/24 rows = 10cm (4") in stockinette stitch after blocking

Blacker Yarns
Tamar DK

 COLOUR A

 COLOUR B

COLOUR C

QUILL NOTES

This shawl is knit from the top down.

The shawl is triangular in shape and increases are made at the edges and in the middle. Four stitches are increased each RS row (both RS edges and 1 st on either side of the centre stitch). Two stitches are increased each WS row (1 st on each WS edge).

The percentages given are calculated based on the percentage of total stitches in the shawl. This can help guide you regarding how much yarn you need. E.g. if you weigh your yarn at the beginning and then at 10%, it will give you an indication of how much yarn you will need in total.

The pattern is written line-by-line in the checklist format.

The border is also charted from row 99 to the end.

Yarn: Blacker Yarn Tamar DK

One Size

ROW	COLOUR	DIRECTIONS	TOTAL STITCHES	% DONE
	A	Cast on 5 sts	5	
1		[RS] Knit all sts	5	
2		[WS] Knit all sts	5	
3		[RS] K1, kfb, k1, kfb, k1	7	
4		[WS] Knit	7	
5		[RS] K1, kfb, k3, kfb, k1	9	
6		[WS] K2, purl to 2 sts before end, k2	9	
7		[RS] K3, yo, k1, M1R, PM, k1, M1L, k1, yo, k3	13	
8		[WS] K2, p1, yo, purl to last 3 sts, yo, p1, k2	15	
9		[RS] K3, yo, knit to marker, M1R, SM, k1, M1L, knit to last 3 sts, yo, k3 **(and every RS row unless otherwise stated)**	19	
10		[WS] K2, p1, yo, purl to last 3 sts, yo, p1, k2 **(and every WS row unless otherwise stated)**	21	
11		[RS]	25	
12		[WS]	27	
13		[RS]	31	
14		[WS]	33	
15		[RS]	37	
16		[WS]	39	
17		[RS]	43	
18		[WS]	45	
19	B	[RS]	49	
20		[WS]	51	
21	A	[RS]	55	
22		[WS]	57	
23	B	[RS] C	61	
24		[WS]	63	
25	A	[RS]	67	
26		[WS]	69	
27	B	[RS] C	73	
28		[WS]	75	
29	A	[RS]	79	
30		[WS]	81	
31	C	[RS]	85	5%

ROW	COLOUR	DIRECTIONS	TOTAL STITCHES	% DONE
32		[WS] K2, p1, yo, knit to last 3 sts, yo, p1, k2	87	
33	A	[RS]	91	
34		[WS]	93	
35	B	[RS]	97	
36		[WS]	99	
37	A	[RS]	103	
38		[WS]	105	
39	B	[RS]	109	
40		[WS]	111	
41	A	[RS]	115	
42		[WS]	117	
43	B	[RS]	121	10%
44		[WS]	123	
45	A	[RS]	127	
46		[WS]	129	
47	C	[RS]	133	
48		[WS] K2, p1, yo, knit to last 3 sts, yo, p1, k2	135	
49	A	[RS]	139	
50		[WS]	141	
51	B	[RS]	145	
52		[WS]	147	15%
53	A	[RS]	151	
54		[WS]	153	
55	B	[RS]	157	
56		[WS]	159	
57	A	[RS]	163	
58		[WS]	165	
59	B	[RS]	169	20%
60		[WS]	171	
61	A	[RS]	175	
62		[WS]	177	
63	C	[RS]	181	
64		[WS] K2, p1, yo, knit to last 3 sts, yo, p1, k2	183	
65	A	[RS]	187	
66		[WS]	189	25%
67	B	[RS]	193	
68		[WS]	195	

One Size

ROW	COLOUR	DIRECTIONS	TOTAL STITCHES	% DONE
69	A	[RS]	199	
70		[WS]	201	
71	B	[RS] C	205	
72		[WS]	207	30%
73	A	[RS]	211	
74		[WS]	213	
75	B	[RS]	217	
76		[WS]	219	
77	A	[RS]	223	
78		[WS]	225	35%
79	C	[RS]	229	
80		[WS] K2, p1, yo, knit to last 3 sts, yo, p1, k2	231	
81	A	[RS] Colour A	235	
82		[WS]	237	
83		[RS]	241	40%
84		[WS]	243	
85	A	[RS]	247	
86		[WS]	249	
87	B	[RS]	253	
88		[WS]	255	45%
89	A	[RS]	259	
90		[WS]	261	
91	B	[RS]	265	
92		[WS]	267	50%
93	A	[RS]	271	
94		[WS]	273	
95	C	[RS]	277	
96		[WS] K2, p1, yo, knit to last 3 sts, yo, p1, k2	279	
97	B	[RS]	283	55%
98		[WS] K2, p1, yo, knit to last 3 sts, yo, p1, k2	285	
99	C	[RS] K3, yo, k1, k2tog, yo, *k2, k2tog, yo* to marker, M1R, SM, k1, M1L, *yo, ssk, k2* to last 6 sts, yo, ssk, k1, yo, k3	289	
100		[WS]	291	

ROW	COLOUR	DIRECTIONS	TOTAL STITCHES	% DONE
101		[RS] K3, yo, *k2, k2tog, yo* to 2 sts before marker, k2, M1R, SM, k1, M1L, k2 *yo, ssk, k2* to last 3 sts, yo, k3	295	60%
102		[WS]	297	
103		[RS] K3, yo, k1, *k2, k2tog, yo* to marker, M1R, SM, k1, M1L, *yo, ssk, k2* to last 4 sts, k1, yo, k3	301	
104		[WS]	303	
105		[RS] K3, yo, k2, *k2, k2tog, yo* to 2 sts before marker, k2, M1R, SM, k1, M1L, k2 *yo, ssk, k2* to last 5 sts, k2, yo, k3	307	65%
106		[WS]	309	
107		[RS] K3, yo, k1, k2tog, yo, *k2, k2tog, yo* to marker, M1R, SM, k1, M1L, *yo, ssk, k2* to last 6 sts, yo, ssk, k1, yo, k3	313	
108		[WS] K2, p1, yo, knit to last 3 sts, yo, p1, k2	315	
109	B	[RS]	319	70%
110		[WS] K2, p1, yo, knit to last 3 sts, yo, p1, k2	321	
111	C	Colour C [RS] K3, yo, k1, *k2, k2tog, yo* to marker, M1R, SM, k1, M1L, *yo, ssk, k2* to last 4 sts, k1, yo, k3	325	
112		[WS]	327	75%
113		[RS] K3, yo, k2, *k2, k2tog, yo* to 2 sts before marker, k2, M1R, SM, k1, M1L, k2 *yo, ssk, k2* to last 5 sts, k2, yo, k3	331	
114		[WS]	333	
115		[RS] K3, yo, k1, k2tog, yo, *k2, k2tog, yo* to marker, M1R, SM, k1, M1L, *yo, ssk, k2* to last 6 sts, yo, ssk, k1, yo, k3	337	
116		[WS] K2, p1, yo, knit to last 3 sts, yo, p1, k2	339	80%
117		[RS] Colour B	343	

ROW	COLOUR	DIRECTIONS	TOTAL STITCHES	% DONE
118		[WS] K2, p1, yo, knit to last 3 sts, yo, p1, k2	345	
119	C	[RS] K3, yo, k1, *k2, k2tog, yo* to marker, M1R, SM, k1, M1L, *yo, ssk, k2* to last 4 sts, k1, yo, k3	349	85%
120		[WS]	351	
121		[RS] K3, yo, k2, *k2, k2tog, yo* to 2 sts before marker, k2, M1R, SM, k1, M1L, k2 *yo, ssk, k2* to last 5 sts, k2, yo, k3	355	
122		[WS]	357	
123	B	[RS] K3, yo, k1, k2tog, yo, *k2, k2tog, yo* to marker, M1R, SM, k1, M1L, *yo, ssk, k2* to last 6 sts, yo, ssk, k1, yo, k3	361	90%
124		[WS]	363	
125		[RS] K3, yo, *k2, k2tog, yo* to 2 sts before marker, k2, M1R, SM, k1, M1L, k2 *yo, ssk, k2* to last 3 sts, yo, k3	367	
126		[WS] K2, p1, yo, k1, *k3, p1* to marker, SM, k3, *p1, k3* to last 4 sts, k1, yo, p1, k2	369	95%
127		[RS] K3, yo, p2, *p3, k1* to 3 sts before marker, p3, SM, k1, p3, *k1, p3* to last 5 sts, p2, yo, K3	371	
		Cast off loosely in rib pattern		100%

Yarn: Blacker Yarn Tamar DK

Charts

Charts are read from bottom to top. They are read right to left on right side rows, and left to right on wrong side rows.

CHART KEY

☐	knit on RS, purl on WS
☐•	purl on RS, knit on WS
☐O	yo
☐/	k2tog
☐\	ssk
R	M1R
L	M1L
☐	no stitch
☐	pattern repeat

Yarn: Blacker Yarn Tamar DK

CHART A

Corresponds to rows 99–102 in written directions.
Colour C: Work chart A once

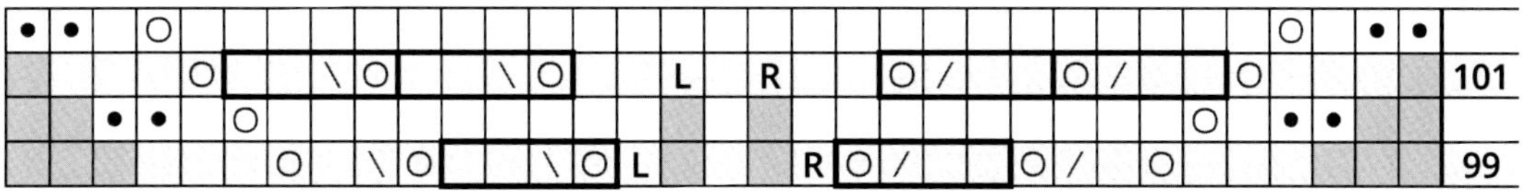

(chart A grid — rows 99 and 101)

CHART B

Corresponds to rows 103–123 in written directions. Work as follows:

Colour C: Work rows 1–6
Colour B: Work rows 7–8

Repeat above once more, then:

Colour C: Work rows 1–4
Colour B: Work row 5 *only*

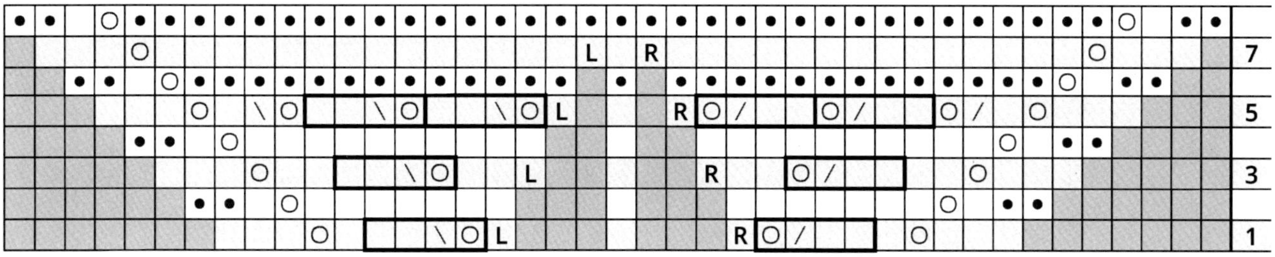

(chart B grid — rows 1, 3, 5, 7)

CHART C

Corresponds to rows 124–127 in written directions.
Colour B: Work chart C once

Cast off loosely in rib pattern

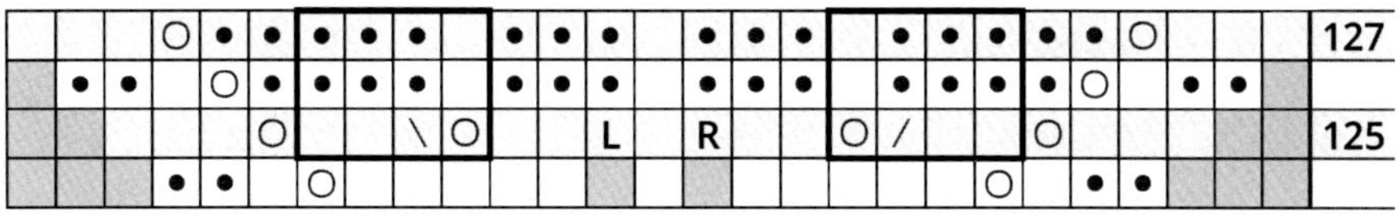

(chart C grid — rows 125 and 127)

FINISHING

Weave in ends.

BLOCKING

For detailed blocking instructions see page 82.

AURORAE
Shawl

Aurorae are the spellbinding flames of light that gather in the sky at both ends of the earth. In the far north, in Finland, it's said that the Aurora Borealis, the Northern Lights, occur when a great arctic fox brushes sparks from the mountain tops with his huge fluffy tail.

On the other side of the planet, the Aboriginal Australians believed that the Aurora Australis, or Southern Lights, were fires from the spirit world: the raging bushfires of sky spirits or the glow of their ancestors' campfires.

I love the idea that people from different places can look at one phenomenon and interpret it so differently and creatively. In a much smaller way we can see this same magic happening in something as simple as a knitting pattern, when the gifted imaginations and hands of knitters from every corner of the world create their own versions of a beautiful object.

The Aurorae Shawl gathers up the strands of that sense of wonder, with rippling shifts of colour and flickering eyelet lace. This shawl was designed using a six colour gradient set, with both sport weight and fingering weight versions. If you're knitting from stash, this is a wonderful way to use up leftovers from other projects: just pick six colours that blend or play well together. This asymmetrical shawl features garter, eyelet and slip stitches: it looks intricate and complicated, but in fact it's a gentle, easy knit. An i-cord edge gives Aurorae a lovely, polished finish.

Size Medium Yarn The Copper Corgi Gradient Mini Skein Set

Size: Large Yarn: Seven Sisters Arts – Meridian Gradient Set

SPECIFICATIONS

SIZE

Medium, Large

FINISHED MEASUREMENTS

Medium

142cm (56") across wingspan
i-cord edge
109cm (43") across picot bind
off edge

Large

157cm (62") across wingspan
i-cord edge
122cm (48") across picot bind
off edge

YARN

Medium

The Copper Corgi Gradient Mini
Skein Set [100% Superwash Merino,
330m/360yds per approx. 113g
set of 6 minis; approx. 55m/60yds
per mini skein], 2 sets
Colourway: Peacock

Sample used approximately
12 mini skeins (6 different colours)
x 45m/50yds each, totalling
540m/600yds in sport weight yarn

Large

Seven Sisters Arts – Meridian
Gradient Set [75% Superwash
Merino, 25% nylon, 823m/900yds
per 200g set of 6 minis;
137m/150yds per 30g mini skein],
1 set
Colourway: Raven's Wing
Sample used approximately
6 mini skeins x 114m/125 yds each
per 25g, totalling 685m/750yds in
fingering weight yarn

NEEDLES

Medium

4.5mm (US 7), 100cm (40")
long circular needles (or size to
obtain gauge)

Large

4mm (US 6), 100cm (40")
long circular needles (or size to
obtain gauge)

NOTIONS

Tapestry needle

GAUGE

Medium

18 sts/30 rows = 10cm (4")
in garter stitch after blocking

Large

22 sts/42 rows = 10cm (4")
in garter stitch after blocking

Gauge is not critical for this shawl,
but a different gauge might result in
a different yardage being required.

AURORAE NOTES

This shawl is an asymmetrical shape and is worked from the tip to the picot cast off at the border. The neck edge has an i-cord border.

The percentages given are calculated based on the percentage of total stitches in the shawl. This can help guide you regarding how much yarn you need. E.g. if you weigh

your yarn at the beginning and then at 10%, it will give you an indication of how much yarn you will need in total.

When casting on, leave approximately 20cm (8") for your tail so that once you have completed your shawl, you can weave it into your i-cord border to create a neat finish at the tip of the shawl.

Follow the colour changes as indicated in the Colour column in the directions checklist. For the striped sections with B and C, carry the yarn not in use up the side then break it where indicated. Do the same for D and E.

COLOURS

With your gradient set arrange your colours from lightest to darkest.

Number them 1–6 lightest to darkest.

Ignore the labelling of your gradient set and relabel them with the letters A–F as follows. These are the labels used for each colour in the directions.

This arrangement is designed to give the most contrast for the two sections in the middle where two colours are used together.

	Lightest to Darkest	Copper Corgi – Peacock	Seven Sisters Arts – Raven's Wing	
1				COLOUR B
2				COLOUR E
3				COLOUR A
4				COLOUR F
5				COLOUR C
6				COLOUR D

Yarn: Copper Corgi – Peacock

Yarn: Seven Sisters Arts – Raven's Wing

Yarn: Seven Sisters Arts – Meridian Gradient Set

Medium

ROW	COLOUR	DIRECTIONS	TOTAL STITCHES	% DONE
	A	Cast on 3 sts (using knitted or long tail cast on method)	3	
1		[RS] KSK	3	
2		[WS] SKS	3	
3		[RS] KSK	3	
4		[WS] Cast on 1 st using backwards loop method, kfb (into cast on st), SKS	5	
5		[RS] KSK, yo, k2	6	
6		[WS] K2, yo, k1, SKS	7	
7		[RS] KSK, yo, k to end	8	
8		[WS] K4, yo, k1, SKS	9	
9		[RS] KSK, yo, k to last 3 sts, k2tog, k1 **(and all following RS rows unless otherwise stated)**	9	
10		[WS] Knit to last 4 sts, yo, k1, SKS **(and all following WS rows unless otherwise stated)**	10	
11		[RS]	10	
12		[WS]	11	
13		[RS]	11	
14		[WS]	12	
15		[RS]	12	
16		[WS]	13	
17		[RS]	13	
18		[WS]	14	
19		[RS]	14	
20		[WS]	15	
21		[RS]	15	
22		[WS]	16	
23		[RS]	16	
24		[WS]	17	
25		[RS]	17	
26		[WS]	18	
27		[RS]	18	

ROW	COLOUR	DIRECTIONS	TOTAL STITCHES	% DONE
28		[WS]	19	
29		[RS]	19	
30		[WS]	20	
31		[RS]	20	
32		[WS]	21	
33		[RS]	21	
34		[WS]	22	
35		[RS]	22	
36		[WS]	23	
37		[RS]	23	
38		[WS]	24	
39		[RS]	24	
40		[WS]	25	
41		[RS]	25	
42		[WS]	26	
43		[RS]	26	
44		[WS]	27	
45		[RS]	27	
46		[WS]	28	
47		[RS]	28	
48		[WS]	29	
49		[RS]	29	
50		[WS]	30	
51		[RS]	30	
52		[WS]	31	
53		[RS]	31	
54		[WS]	32	
55		[RS]	32	
56		[WS]	33	
57		[RS]	33	
58		[WS]	34	
59		[RS]	34	
60		[WS]	35	5%
61		[RS]	35	
62		[WS]	36	
63		[RS]	36	

ROW	COLOUR	DIRECTIONS	TOTAL STITCHES	% DONE
64		[WS]	37	
65		[RS]	37	
66		[WS]	38	
67		[RS]	38	
68		[WS]	39	
69		[RS]	39	
70		[WS]	40	
71		[RS]	40	
72		[WS]	41	
73		[RS]	41	
74		[WS]	42	
75		[RS]	42	
76		[WS]	43	
77		[RS]	43	
78		[WS]	44	
79		[RS]	44	
80		[WS]	45	
81		[RS]	45	
82		[WS]	46	
83		[RS]	46	
84		[WS]	47	
85		[RS]	47	
86		[WS]	48	
87		[RS]	48	
88		[WS]	49	10%
89		[RS]	49	
90		[WS]	50	
91		[RS]	50	
92		[WS]	51	
93		[RS]	51	
94		[WS]	52	
95		[RS]	52	
96		[WS]	53	
97		[RS]	53	
98		[WS]	54	
99		[RS]	54	

ROW	COLOUR	DIRECTIONS	TOTAL STITCHES	% DONE
100		[WS]	55	
101		[RS]	55	
102		[WS]	56	
103		[RS]	56	
104		[WS]	57	
105		[RS]	57	
106		[WS]	58	
107		[RS]	58	
108		[WS]	59	
109		[RS]	59	
110		[WS]	60	15%
111		[RS]	60	
112		[WS]	61	
113		[RS]	61	
114		[WS]	62	
115		[RS]	62	
116		[WS]	63	
117		[RS]	63	
118		[WS]	64	
119		[RS]	64	
120		[WS]	65	
121		[RS]	65	
122		[WS] At end of this row break colour A yarn	66	
123	B	[RS]	66	
124		[WS]	67	
125	C	[RS] KSK, yo, k9, *sl1, k5* to last 7 sts, sl1, k3, k2tog, k1	67	
126		[WS] K5, sl1 wyf, *k5, sl1 wyf * to last 13 sts, k9, yo, k1, SKS	68	
127	B	[RS]	68	
128		[WS]	69	20%
129	C	[RS]	69	
130		[WS]	70	
131	B	[RS]	70	
132		[WS]	71	

Medium

ROW	COLOUR	DIRECTIONS	TOTAL STITCHES	% DONE
133	C	[RS] KSK, yo, k8, *sl1, k5* to last 6 sts, sl1, k2, k2tog, k1	71	
134		[WS] K4, sl1 wyf, *k5, sl1 wyf* to last 12 sts, k8, yo, k1, SKS	72	
135	B	[RS]	72	
136		[WS]	73	
137	C	[RS]	73	
138		[WS]	74	
139	B	[RS]	74	
140		[WS]	75	
141	C	[RS] KSK, yo, k7, *sl1, k5* to last 5 sts, k2, k2tog, k1	75	
142		[WS] K4, *k5, sl1 wyf* to last 11 sts, k7, yo, k1, SKS	76	
143	B	[RS]	76	
144		[WS]	77	25%
145	C	[RS]	77	
146		[WS]	78	
147	B	[RS]	78	
148		[WS]	79	
149	C	[RS] KSK, yo, k6, *sl1, k5* to last 4 sts, k1, k2tog, k1	79	
150		[WS] K3, *k5, sl1 wyf* to last 10 sts, k6, yo, k1, SKS	80	
151	B	[RS]	80	
152		[WS]	81	
153	C	[RS]	81	
154		[WS]	82	
155	B	[RS]	82	
156		[WS]	83	
157	C	[RS] KSK, yo, k5, *sl1, k5* to last 3 sts, k2tog, k1	83	
158		[WS] K2, *k5, sl1 wyf* to last 9 sts, k5, yo, k1, SKS	84	
159	B	[RS]	84	30%
160		[WS]	85	
161	C	[RS]	85	
162		[WS]	86	

ROW	COLOUR	DIRECTIONS	TOTAL STITCHES	% DONE
163	B	[RS]	86	
164		[WS]	87	
165	C	[RS] KSK, yo, k4, *sl1, k5* to last 8 sts, sl1, k4, k2tog, k1	87	
166		[WS] K6, sl1 wyf, *k5, sl1 wyf* to last 8 sts, k4, yo, k1, SKS	88	
167	B	[RS]	88	
168		[WS]	89	
169	C	[RS]	89	
170		[WS]	90	
171	B	[RS]	90	
172		[WS]	91	
173	C	[RS] KSK, yo, k9, *sl1, k5* to last 7 sts, sl1, k3, k2tog, k1	91	35%
174		[WS] K5, sl1 wyf, *k5, sl1 wyf * to last 13 sts, k9, yo, k1, SKS	92	
175	B	[RS]	92	
176		[WS]	93	
177	C	[RS]	93	
178		[WS]	94	
179	B	[RS]	94	
180		[WS]	95	
181	C	[RS] KSK, yo, k8, *sl1, k5* to last 6 sts, sl1, k2, k2tog, k1	95	
182		[WS] K4, sl1 wyf, *k5, sl1 wyf* to last 12 sts, k8, yo, k1, SKS	96	
183	B	[RS]	96	
184		[WS]	97	
185	C	[RS]	97	40%
186		[WS]	98	
187	B	[RS]	98	
188		[WS]	99	
189	C	[RS] KSK, yo, k7, *sl1, k5* to last 5 sts, k2, k2tog, k1	99	
190		[WS] K4, *k5, sl1 wyf* to last 11 sts, k7, yo, k1, SKS	100	

ROW	COLOUR	DIRECTIONS	TOTAL STITCHES	% DONE
191	B	[RS]	100	
192		[WS]	101	
193	C	[RS]	101	
194		[WS]	102	
195	B	[RS]	102	
196		[WS]	103	
197	C	[RS] KSK, yo, k6, *sl1, k5* to last 4 sts, k1, k2tog, k1	103	45%
198		[WS] K3, *k5, sl1 wyf* to last 10 sts, k6, yo, k1, SKS	104	
199	B	[RS]	104	
200		[WS]	105	
201	C	[RS]	105	
202		[WS]	106	
203	B	[RS]	106	
204		[WS]	107	
205	C	[RS] KSK, yo, k5, *sl1, k5* to last 3 sts, k2tog, k1	107	
206		[WS] K2, *k5, sl1 wyf* to last 9 sts, k5, yo, k1, SKS	108	
207	B	[RS]	108	
208		[WS] At end of this row break colours B & C yarns	109	50%
209	D	[RS]	109	
210		[WS]	110	
211		[RS] KSK, yo, k2, *yo, k2tog* to last 3 sts, k2tog, k1	110	
212		[WS]	111	
213	E	[RS]	111	
214		[WS]	112	
215	D	[RS] KSK, yo, k6, *sl1, k5* to last 7 sts, sl1, k3, k2tog, k1	112	
216		[WS] K5, sl1 wyf, *k5, sl1 wyf* to last 10 sts, k6, yo, k1, SKS	113	
217	E	[RS]	113	
218		[WS]	114	
219	D	[RS]	114	55%

ROW	COLOUR	DIRECTIONS	TOTAL STITCHES	% DONE
220		[WS]	115	
221		[RS] KSK, yo, k1, *yo, k2tog* to last 3 sts, k2tog, k1	115	
222		[WS]	116	
223	E	[RS]	116	
224		[WS]	117	
225	D	[RS] KSK, yo, k7, *sl1, k5* to last 5 sts, k2, k2tog, k1	117	
226		[WS] K4, *k5, sl1 wyf* to last 11 sts, k7, yo, k1, SKS	118	
227	E	[RS]	118	
228		[WS]	119	
229	D	[RS]	119	60%
230		[WS]	120	
231		[RS] KSK, yo, k2, *yo, k2tog* to last 3 sts, k2tog, k1	120	
232		[WS]	121	
233	E	[RS]	121	
234		[WS]	122	
235	D	[RS] KSK, yo, k8, *sl1, k5* to last 3 sts, k2tog, k1	122	
236		[WS] K2, *k5, sl1 wyf* to last 12 sts, k8, yo, k1, SKS	123	
237	E	[RS]	123	
238		[WS]	124	
239	D	[RS]	124	65%
240		[WS]	125	
241		[RS] KSK, yo, k1, *yo, k2tog* to last 3 sts, k2tog, k1	125	
242		[WS]	126	
243	E	[RS]	126	
244		[WS]	127	
245	D	[RS] KSK, yo, k9, *sl1, k5* to last 7 sts, sl1, k3, k2tog, k1	127	
246		[WS] K5, sl1 wyf, *k5, sl1 wyf * to last 13 sts, k9, yo, k1, SKS	128	
247	E	[RS]	128	

Medium

ROW	COLOUR	DIRECTIONS	TOTAL STITCHES	% DONE
248		[WS]	129	70%
249	D	[RS]	129	
250		[WS]	130	
251		[RS] KSK, yo, k2, *yo, k2tog* to last 3 sts, k2tog, k1	130	
252		[WS]	131	
253	E	[RS]	131	
254		[WS]	132	
255	D	[RS] KSK, yo, k4, *sl1, k5* to last 5 sts, k2, k2tog, k1	132	
256		[WS] K4, *k5, sl1 wyf* to last 8 sts, k4, yo, k1, SKS	133	
257	E	[RS]	133	75%
258		[WS]	134	
259	D	[RS]	134	
260		[WS]	135	
261		[RS] KSK, yo, k1, *yo, k2tog* to last 3 sts, k2tog, k1	135	
262		[WS] At end of this row break colours D & E yarns	136	
263	F	[RS]	136	
264		[WS]	137	
265		[RS]	137	
266		[WS]	138	80%
267		[RS]	138	
268		[WS]	139	
269		[RS]	139	
270		[WS]	140	
271		[RS]	140	
272		[WS]	141	
273		[RS]	141	
274		[WS]	142	85%
275		[RS]	142	
276		[WS]	143	
277		[RS]	143	
278		[WS]	144	

ROW	COLOUR	DIRECTIONS	TOTAL STITCHES	% DONE
279		[RS]	144	
280		[WS]	145	
281		[RS]	145	
282		[WS]	146	
283		[RS]	146	90%
284		[WS]	147	
285		[RS]	147	
286		[WS]	148	
287		[RS]	148	
288		[WS]	149	
289	E	[RS]	149	
290		[WS]	150	
291		[RS] KSK, yo, k2, *yo, k2tog* to last 3 sts, k2tog, k1	150	95%
292		[WS]	151	
293	F	[RS]	151	
294		[WS] At end of this row break colour F yarn	152	
295	E	[RS]	152	
		Picot cast off: Cast off 2 sts, *slip st back onto left needle, cast on 2 sts using knitting cast on method, cast off 5 sts* repeat to 2 sts before the end, cast off final 2 sts		100%

Large

AURORAE

ROW	COLOUR	DIRECTIONS	TOTAL STITCHES	% DONE
	A	Cast on 3 sts (using knitted or long tail cast on method)	3	
1		[RS] KSK	3	
2		[WS] SKS	3	
3		[RS] KSK	3	
4		[WS] Cast on 1 st using backwards loop method, kfb (into cast on st), SKS	5	
5		[RS] KSK, yo, k2	6	
6		[WS] K2, yo, k1, SKS	7	
7		[RS] KSK, yo, k to end	8	
8		[WS] K4, yo, k1, SKS	9	
9		[RS] KSK, yo, k to last 3 sts, k2tog, k1 **(and all following RS rows unless otherwise stated)**	9	
10		[WS] Knit to last 4 sts, yo, k1, SKS **(and all following WS rows unless otherwise stated)**	10	
11		[RS]	10	
12		[WS]	11	
13		[RS]	11	
14		[WS]	12	
15		[RS]	12	
16		[WS]	13	
17		[RS]	13	
18		[WS]	14	
19		[RS]	14	
20		[WS]	15	
21		[RS]	15	
22		[WS]	16	
23		[RS]	16	
24		[WS]	17	
25		[RS]	17	

ROW	COLOUR	DIRECTIONS	TOTAL STITCHES	% DONE
26		[WS]	18	
27		[RS]	18	
28		[WS]	19	
29		[RS]	19	
30		[WS]	20	
31		[RS]	20	
32		[WS]	21	
33		[RS]	21	
34		[WS]	22	
35		[RS]	22	
36		[WS]	23	
37		[RS]	23	
38		[WS]	24	
39		[RS]	24	
40		[WS]	25	
41		[RS]	25	
42		[WS]	26	
43		[RS]	26	
44		[WS]	27	
45		[RS]	27	
46		[WS]	28	
47		[RS]	28	
48		[WS]	29	
49		[RS]	29	
50		[WS]	30	
51		[RS]	30	
52		[WS]	31	
53		[RS]	31	
54		[WS]	32	
55		[RS]	32	
56		[WS]	33	
57		[RS]	33	
58		[WS]	34	
59		[RS]	34	

Large

ROW	COLOUR	DIRECTIONS	TOTAL STITCHES	% DONE
60		[WS]	35	
61		[RS]	35	
62		[WS]	36	
63		[RS]	36	
64		[WS]	37	
65		[RS]	37	
66		[WS]	38	
67		[RS]	38	
68		[WS]	39	
69		[RS]	39	
70		[WS]	40	
71		[RS]	40	
72		[WS]	41	
73		[RS]	41	
74		[WS]	42	5%
75		[RS]	42	
76		[WS]	43	
77		[RS]	43	
78		[WS]	44	
79		[RS]	44	
80		[WS]	45	
81		[RS]	45	
82		[WS]	46	
83		[RS]	46	
84		[WS]	47	
85		[RS]	47	
86		[WS]	48	
87		[RS]	48	
88		[WS]	49	
89		[RS]	49	
90		[WS]	50	
91		[RS]	50	
92		[WS]	51	
93		[RS]	51	

ROW	COLOUR	DIRECTIONS	TOTAL STITCHES	% DONE
94		[WS]	52	
95		[RS]	52	
96		[WS]	53	
97		[RS]	53	
98		[WS]	54	
99		[RS]	54	
100		[WS]	55	
101		[RS]	55	
102		[WS]	56	
103		[RS]	56	
104		[WS]	57	
105		[RS]	57	
106		[WS]	58	
107		[RS]	58	
108		[WS]	59	
109		[RS]	59	10%
110		[WS]	60	
111		[RS]	60	
112		[WS]	61	
113		[RS]	61	
114		[WS]	62	
115		[RS]	62	
116		[WS]	63	
117		[RS]	63	
118		[WS]	64	
119		[RS]	64	
120		[WS]	65	
121		[RS]	65	
122		[WS]	66	
123		[RS]	66	
124		[WS]	67	
125		[RS]	67	
126		[WS]	68	
127		[RS]	68	

ROW	COLOUR	DIRECTIONS	TOTAL STITCHES	% DONE
128		[WS]	69	
129		[RS]	69	
130		[WS]	70	
131		[RS]	70	
132		[WS]	71	
133		[RS]	71	
134		[WS]	72	
135		[RS]	72	15%
136		[WS]	73	
137		[RS]	73	
138		[WS]	74	
139		[RS]	74	
140		[WS]	75	
141		[RS]	75	
142		[WS]	76	
143		[RS]	76	
144		[WS]	77	
145		[RS]	77	
146		[WS] At end of this row break colour A yarn	78	
147	B	[RS]	78	
148		[WS]	79	
149	C	[RS] KSK, yo, k6, *sl1, k5* to last 4 sts, k1, k2tog, k1	79	
150		[WS] K3, *k5, sl1 wyf* to last 10 sts, k6, yo, k1, SKS	80	
151	B	[RS]	80	
152		[WS]	81	
153	C	[RS]	81	
154		[WS]	82	
155	B	[RS]	82	
156		[WS]	83	

ROW	COLOUR	DIRECTIONS	TOTAL STITCHES	% DONE
157	C	[RS] KSK, yo, k5, *sl1, k5* to last 3 sts, k2tog, k1	83	
158		[WS] K2, *k5, sl1 wyf* to last 9 sts, k5, yo, k1, SKS	84	20%
159	B	[RS]	84	
160		[WS]	85	
161	C	[RS]	85	
162		[WS]	86	
163	B	[RS]	86	
164		[WS]	87	
165	C	[RS] KSK, yo, k4, *sl1, k5* to last 8 sts, sl1, k4, k2tog, k1	87	
166		[WS] K6, sl1 wyf, *k5, sl1 wyf* to last 8 sts, k4, yo, k1, SKS	88	
167	B	[RS]	88	
168		[WS]	89	
169	C	[RS]	89	
170		[WS]	90	
171	B	[RS]	90	
172		[WS]	91	
173	C	[RS] KSK, yo, k9, *sl1, k5* to last 7 sts, sl1, k3, k2tog, k1	91	
174		[WS] K5, sl1 wyf, *k5, sl1 wyf * to last 13 sts, k9, yo, k1, SKS	92	
175	B	[RS]	92	
176		[WS]	93	
177	C	[RS]	93	25%
178		[WS]	94	
179	B	[RS]	94	
180		[WS]	95	
181	C	[RS] KSK, yo, k8, *sl1, k5* to last 6 sts, sl1, k2, k2tog, k1	95	

Large

ROW	COLOUR	DIRECTIONS	TOTAL STITCHES	% DONE
182		[WS] K4, sl1 wyf, *k5, sl1 wyf* to last 12 sts, k8, yo, k1, SKS	96	
183	B	[RS]	96	
184		[WS]	97	
185	C	[RS]	97	
186		[WS]	98	
187	B	[RS]	98	
188		[WS]	99	
189	C	[RS] KSK, yo, k7, *sl1, k5* to last 5 sts, k2, k2tog, k1	99	
190		[WS] K4, *k5, sl1 wyf* to last 11 sts, k7, yo, k1, SKS	100	
191	B	[RS]	100	
192		[WS]	101	
193	C	[RS]	101	
194		[WS]	102	
195	B	[RS]	102	30%
196		[WS]	103	
197	C	[RS] KSK, yo, k6, *sl1, k5* to last 4 sts, k1, k2tog, k1	103	
198		[WS] K3, *k5, sl1 wyf* to last 10 sts, k6, yo, k1, SKS	104	
199	B	[RS]	104	
200		[WS]	105	
201	C	[RS]	105	
202		[WS]	106	
203	B	[RS]	106	
204		[WS]	107	
205	C	[RS] KSK, yo, k5, *sl1, k5* to last 3 sts, k2tog, k1	107	
206		[WS] K2, *k5, sl1 wyf* to last 9 sts, k5, yo, k1, SKS	108	
207	B	[RS]	108	

ROW	COLOUR	DIRECTIONS	TOTAL STITCHES	% DONE
208		[WS]	109	
209	C	[RS]	109	
210		[WS]	110	
211	B	[RS]	110	
212		[WS]	111	35%
213	C	[RS] KSK, yo, k4, *sl1, k5* to last 8 sts, sl1, k4, k2tog, k1	111	
214		[WS] K6, sl1 wyf *k5, sl1 wyf* to last 8 sts, k4, yo, k1, SKS	112	
215	B	[RS]	112	
216		[WS]	113	
217	C	[RS]	113	
218		[WS]	114	
219	B	[RS]	114	
220		[WS]	115	
221	C	[RS] KSK, yo, k9, *sl1, k5* to last 7 sts, sl1, k3, k2tog, k1	115	
222		[WS] K5, sl1 wyf, *k5, sl1 wyf * to last 13 sts, k9, yo, k1, SKS	116	
223	B	[RS]	116	
224		[WS]	117	
225	C	[RS]	117	
226		[WS]	118	
227	B	[RS]	118	40%
228		[WS]	119	
229	C	[RS] KSK, yo, k8, *sl1, k5* to last 6 sts, sl1, k2, k2tog, k1	119	
230		[WS] K4, sl1 wyf, *k5, sl1 wyf* to last 12 sts, k8, yo, k1, SKS	120	
231	B	[RS]	120	
232		[WS]	121	
233	C	[RS]	121	
234		[WS]	122	

ROW	COLOUR	DIRECTIONS	TOTAL STITCHES	% DONE
235	B	[RS]	122	
236		[WS]	123	
237	C	[RS] KSK, yo, k7, *sl1, k5* to last 5 sts, k2, k2tog, k1	123	
238		[WS] K4, *k5, sl1 wyf* to last 11 sts, k7, yo, k1, SKS	124	
239	B	[RS]	124	
240		[WS]	125	
241	C	[RS]	125	45%
242		[WS]	126	
243	B	[RS]	126	
244		[WS]	127	
245	C	[RS] KSK, yo, k6, *sl1, k5* to last 4 sts, k1, k2tog, k1	127	
246		[WS] K3, *k5, sl1 wyf* to last 10 sts, k6, yo, k1, SKS	128	
247	B	[RS]	128	
248		[WS] At the end of this row break colours B & C yarns	129	
249	D	[RS]	129	
250		[WS]	130	
251		[RS] KSK, yo, k2, *yo, k2tog* to last 3 sts, k2tog, k1	130	
252		[WS]	131	
253	E	[RS]	131	
254		[WS]	132	
255	D	[RS] KSK, yo, k4, *sl1, k5* to last 5 sts, k2, k2tog, k1	132	50%
256		[WS] K4, *k5, sl1 wyf* to last 8 sts, k4, yo, k1, SKS	133	
257	E	[RS]	133	
258		[WS]	134	
259	D	[RS]	134	

ROW	COLOUR	DIRECTIONS	TOTAL STITCHES	% DONE
260		[WS]	135	
261		[RS] KSK, yo, k1, *yo, k2tog* to last 3 sts, k2tog, k1	135	
262		[WS]	136	
263	E	[RS]	136	
264		[WS]	137	
265	D	[RS] KSK, yo, k5, *sl1, k5* to last 9 sts, sl1, k5, k2tog, k1	137	
266		[WS] K7, sl1 wyf, *k5, sl1 wyf* to last 9 sts, k5, yo, k1, SKS	138	
267	E	[RS]	138	
268		[WS]	139	55%
269	D	[RS]	139	
270		[WS]	140	
271		[RS] KSK, yo, k2, *yo, k2tog* to last 3 sts, k2tog, k1	140	
272		[WS]	141	
273	E	[RS]	141	
274		[WS]	142	
275	D	[RS] KSK, yo, k6, *sl1, k5* to last 7 sts, sl1, k3, k2tog, k1	142	
276		[WS] K5, sl1 wyf *k5, sl1 wyf* to last 10 sts, k6, yo, k1, SKS	143	
277	E	[RS]	143	
278		[WS]	144	
279	D	[RS]	144	
280		[WS]	145	60%
281		[RS] KSK, yo, k1, *yo, k2tog* to last 3 sts, k2tog, k1	145	
282		[WS]	146	
283	E	[RS]	146	
284		[WS]	147	

Large

ROW	COLOUR	DIRECTIONS	TOTAL STITCHES	% DONE
285	D	[RS] KSK, yo, k7, *sl1, k5* to last 5 sts, k2, k2tog, k1	147	
286		[WS] K4, *k5, sl1 wyf* to last 11 sts, k7, yo, k1, SKS	148	
287	E	[RS]	148	
288		[WS]	149	
289	D	[RS]	149	
290		[WS]	150	
291		[RS] KSK, yo, k2, *yo, k2tog* to last 3 sts, k2tog, k1	150	
292		[WS]	151	65%
293	E	[RS]	151	
294		[WS]	152	
295	D	[RS] KSK, yo, k8, *sl1, k5* to last 3 sts, k2tog, k1	152	
296		[WS] K2, *k5, sl1 wyf* to last 12 sts, k8, yo, k1, SKS	153	
297	E	[RS]	153	
298		[WS]	154	
299	D	[RS]	154	
300		[WS]	155	
301		[RS] KSK, yo, k1, *yo, k2tog* to last 3 sts, k2tog, k1	155	
302		[WS]	156	
303	E	[RS]	156	70%
304		[WS]	157	
305	D	[RS] KSK, yo, k9, *sl1, k5* to last 7 sts, sl1, k3, k2tog, k1	157	
306		[WS] K5, sl1 wyf, *k5, sl1 wyf * to last 13 sts, k9, yo, k1, SKS	158	
307	E	[RS]	158	
308		[WS]	159	
309	D	[RS]	159	

ROW	COLOUR	DIRECTIONS	TOTAL STITCHES	% DONE
310		[WS]	160	
311		[RS] KSK, yo, k2, *yo, k2tog* to last 3 sts, k2tog, k1	160	
312		[WS]	161	
313	E	[RS]	161	
314		[WS]	162	75%
315	D	[RS] KSK, yo, k4, *sl1, k5* to last 5 sts, k2, k2tog, k1	162	
316		[WS] K4, *k5, sl1 wyf* to last 8 sts, k4, yo, k1, SKS	163	
317	E	[RS]	163	
318		[WS]	164	
319	D	[RS]	164	
320		[WS]	165	
321		[RS] KSK, yo, k1, *yo, k2tog* to last 3 sts, k2tog, k1	165	
322		[WS] At end of this row break colours D & E yarns	166	
323	F	[RS]	166	
324		[WS]	167	
325		[RS]	167	80%
326		[WS]	168	
327		[RS]	168	
328		[WS]	169	
329		[RS]	169	
330		[WS]	170	
331		[RS]	170	
332		[WS]	171	
333		[RS]	171	
334		[WS]	172	
335		[RS]	172	85%
336		[WS]	173	
337		[RS]	173	
338		[WS]	174	

ROW	COLOUR	DIRECTIONS	TOTAL STITCHES	% DONE
339		[RS]	174	
340		[WS]	175	
341		[RS]	175	
342		[WS]	176	
343		[RS]	176	
344		[WS]	177	
345		[RS]	177	90%
346		[WS]	178	
347		[RS]	178	
348		[WS]	179	
349		[RS]	179	
350		[WS]	180	
351		[RS]	180	
352		[WS]	181	
353		[RS]	181	
354		[WS]	182	
355	E	[RS]	182	95%
356		[WS]	183	
357		[RS] KSK, yo, k1, *yo, k2tog* to last 3 sts, k2tog, k1	183	
358		[WS]	184	
359	F	[RS]	184	
360		[WS] At the end of this row break colour F	185	
361	E	[RS]	185	
		Picot cast off: Cast off 2 sts, *slip st back onto left needle, cast on 2 sts using knitting cast on method cast off 5 sts* repeat to 2 sts before the end, cast off final 2 sts		100%

FINISHING

Weave in ends.

BLOCKING

For detailed blocking instructions see page 82.

SONDER
Shawl

The Sonder Shawl is a big, soft, cosy shawl to wrap up the Shawl Society journey. "Sonder" is a new word, originally defined as "the realization that each random passer-by is living a life as vivid and complex as your own." That sudden flash of recognition occurs at random moments.

Yarn: The Fibre Co. Tundra

Sometimes it's brought on by the novelty of a new place: taking a crowded train through a foreign country and watching the evidence of thousands of unknown lives flash by in seconds. Other times, a mundane moment spent standing in a coffee shop queue becomes suddenly mysterious as you wonder about the inner lives of the strangers who surround you.

The moment we meet a new friend, we gain entrance into the rich story of their lives. It is the best way we have of tapping into that abundance of experience, and for the final Shawl Society project I wanted a design that reflected the connection and warmth we share as a community of knitters. The Sonder Shawl is an elongated triangle shape, veering towards a scarf. It has an open, easy to memorise stitch pattern and is finished with playful tassels. In the spirit of sharing, it is wonderful gift knitting: the bulky yarn knits up super fast and the contemporary design will appeal even to shawl sceptics.

SPECIFICATIONS

SIZE
One size

FINISHED MEASUREMENTS
163cm (64") long
66cm (26") across bind off edge

YARN
The Fibre Co Tundra [60% Alpaca, 30% Wool, 10% Silk; 109m/120yds per 100g skein], 3 x skeins,
Colour: Silver Wolf

Sample used all three skeins of Tundra

OR

327m/360 yards of bulky weight yarn

NEEDLES
8mm (US 11), 100cm (40") long circular needles (or size to obtain gauge)

NOTIONS
Tapestry needle

GAUGE
12 sts/16 rows = 10cm (4") in shawl stitch pattern after blocking

Gauge is not critical for this shawl, but a different gauge might result in a different yardage required

Yarn: The Fibre Co Tundra

SONDER NOTES

The percentages given are calculated based on the percentage of total stitches in the shawl. This can help guide you regarding how much yarn you need. E.g. if you weigh your yarn at the beginning and then at 10%, it will give you an indication of how much yarn you will need in total.

This shawl is an elongated triangular shape and is worked from the tip to the cast off at the border.

The dark borders in the directions indicate the 8 row repeat. If you would like to make the shawl bigger you can continue with more repeats.

Yarn: The Fibre Co Tundra

One Size

ROW	DIRECTIONS	TOTAL STITCHES	% DONE
	Cast on 5 sts (knitted cast on or backwards loop)	5	
1	[RS] Knit all sts	5	
2	[WS] Sl1, k4	5	
3	[RS] Knit all sts	5	
4	[WS] Sl1, k4	5	
5	[RS] Knit all sts	5	
6	[WS] Sl1, k4	5	
7	[RS] Knit all stitches; at the end, don't turn to other side, instead turn work 90 degrees right then pick up and knit 3 sts along adjacent edge	8	
8	[WS] Knit all sts	8	
9	[RS] K4, yo, k4	9	
10	[WS] Knit all sts	9	
11	[RS] K4, yo, k1, yo, k4	11	
12	[WS] Knit all sts	11	
13	[RS] K4, yo, k2tog, k1, yo, k4	12	
14	[WS] Knit all sts	12	
15	[RS] K4, yo, k2tog, ssk, yo, k4	12	
16	[WS] Knit all sts	12	
17	[RS] K4, yo, k2tog, k2, yo, k4	13	
18	[WS] Knit all sts	13	
19	[RS] K4, yo, k2tog, k1, ssk, yo, k4	13	
20	[WS] K4, purl to last 4 sts, k4	13	
21	[RS] K4, yo, k2tog, p1, k2, yo, k4	14	
22	[WS] K4, purl to last 4 sts, k4	14	
23	[RS] K4, yo, k2tog, k2, ssk, yo, k4	14	
24	[WS] Knit all sts	14	
25	[RS] K4, yo, *k2tog, yo* to last 4 sts, k4	15	
26	[WS] Knit all sts	15	
27	[RS] K4, yo, k2tog, k3, ssk, yo, k4	15	
28	[WS] K4, purl to last 4 sts, k4	15	
29	[RS] K4, yo, k2tog, *p1, k1* to last 5 sts, k1, yo, k4	16	
30	[WS] K4, purl to last 4 sts, k4	16	
31	[RS] K4, yo, k2tog, knit to last 6 sts, ssk, yo, k4	16	

ROW	DIRECTIONS	TOTAL STITCHES	% DONE
32	[WS] Knit all sts	16	
33	[RS] K4, yo, *k2tog, yo* to last 4 sts, k4	17	
34	[WS] Knit all sts	17	
35	[RS] K4, yo, k2tog, knit to last 6 sts, ssk, yo, k4	17	
36	[WS] K4, purl to last 4 sts, k4	17	5%
37	[RS] K4, yo, k2tog, *p1, k1* to last 5 sts, k1, yo, k4	18	
38	[WS] K4, purl to last 4 sts, k4	18	
39	[RS] K4, yo, k2tog, knit to last 6 sts, ssk, yo, k4	18	
40	[WS] Knit all sts	18	
41	[RS] K4, yo, *k2tog, yo* to last 4 sts, k4	19	
42	[WS] Knit all sts	19	
43	[RS] K4, yo, k2tog, knit to last 6 sts, ssk, yo, k4	19	
44	[WS] K4, purl to last 4 sts, k4	19	
45	[RS] K4, yo, k2tog, *p1, k1* to last 5 sts, k1, yo, k4	20	
46	[WS] K4, purl to last 4 sts, k4	20	
47	[RS] K4, yo, k2tog, knit to last 6 sts, ssk, yo, k4	20	
48	[WS] Knit all sts	20	
49	[RS] K4, yo, *k2tog, yo* to last 4 sts, k4	21	
50	[WS] Knit all sts	21	
51	[RS] K4, yo, k2tog, knit to last 6 sts, ssk, yo, k4	21	
52	[WS] K4, purl to last 4 sts, k4	21	
53	[RS] K4, yo, k2tog, *p1, k1* to last 5 sts, k1, yo, k4	22	
54	[WS] K4, purl to last 4 sts, k4	22	
55	[RS] K4, yo, k2tog, knit to last 6 sts, ssk, yo, k4	22	
56	[WS] Knit all sts	22	
57	[RS] K4, yo, *k2tog, yo* to last 4 sts, k4	23	
58	[WS] Knit all sts	23	10%
59	[RS] K4, yo, k2tog, knit to last 6 sts, ssk, yo, k4	23	
60	[WS] K4, purl to last 4 sts, k4	23	
61	[RS] K4, yo, k2tog, *p1, k1* to last 5 sts, k1, yo, k4	24	

ROW	DIRECTIONS	TOTAL STITCHES	% DONE
62	[WS] K4, purl to last 4 sts, k4	24	
63	[RS] K4, yo, k2tog, knit to last 6 sts, ssk, yo, k4	24	
64	[WS] Knit all sts	24	
65	[RS] K4, yo, *k2tog, yo* to last 4 sts, k4	25	
66	[WS] Knit all sts	25	
67	[RS] K4, yo, k2tog, knit to last 6 sts ssk, yo, k4	25	
68	[WS] K4, purl to last 4 sts, k4	25	
69	[RS] K4, yo, k2tog, *p1, k1* to last 5 sts, k1, yo, k4	26	
70	[WS] K4, purl to last 4 sts, k4	26	
71	[RS] K4, yo, k2tog, knit to last 6 sts, ssk, yo, k4	26	
72	[WS] Knit all sts	26	
73	[RS] K4, yo, *k2tog, yo* to last 4 sts, k4	27	
74	[WS] Knit all sts	27	
75	[RS] K4, yo, k2tog, knit to last 6 sts, ssk, yo, k4	27	
76	[WS] K4, purl to last 4 sts, k4	27	15%
77	[RS] K4, yo, k2tog, *p1, k1* to last 5 sts, k1, yo, k4	28	
78	[WS] K4, purl to last 4 sts, k4	28	
79	[RS] K4, yo, k2tog, knit to last 6 sts, ssk, yo, k4	28	
80	[WS] Knit all sts	28	
81	[RS] K4, yo, *k2tog, yo* to last 4 sts, k4	29	
82	[WS] Knit all sts	29	
83	[RS] K4, yo, k2tog, knit to last 6 sts, ssk, yo, k4	29	
84	[WS] K4, purl to last 4 sts, k4	29	
85	[RS] K4, yo, k2tog, *p1, k1* to last 5 sts, k1, yo, k4	30	
86	[WS] K4, purl to last 4 sts, k4	30	
87	[RS] K4, yo, k2tog, knit to last 6 sts, ssk, yo, k4	30	
88	[WS] Knit all sts	30	
89	[RS] K4, yo, *k2tog, yo* to last 4 sts, k4	31	
90	[WS] Knit all sts	31	
91	[RS] K4, yo, k2tog, knit to last 6 sts, ssk, yo, k4	31	20%

ROW	DIRECTIONS	TOTAL STITCHES	% DONE
92	[WS] K4, purl to last 4 sts, k4	31	
93	[RS] K4, yo, k2tog, *p1, k1* to last 5 sts, k1, yo, k4	32	
94	[WS] K4, purl to last 4 sts, k4	32	
95	[RS] K4, yo, k2tog, knit to last 6 sts, ssk, yo, k4	32	
96	[WS] Knit all sts	32	
97	[RS] K4, yo, *k2tog, yo* to last 4 sts, k4	33	
98	[WS] Knit all sts	33	
99	[RS] K4, yo, k2tog, knit to last 6 sts, ssk, yo, k4	33	
100	[WS] K4, purl to last 4 sts, k4	33	
101	[RS] K4, yo, k2tog, *p1, k1* to last 5 sts, k1, yo, k4	34	
102	[WS] K4, purl to last 4 sts, k4	34	
103	[RS] K4, yo, k2tog, knit to last 6 sts, ssk, yo, k4	34	
104	[WS] Knit all sts	34	
105	[RS] K4, yo, *k2tog, yo* to last 4 sts, k4	35	25%
106	[WS] Knit all sts	35	
107	[RS] K4, yo, k2tog, knit to last 6 sts, ssk, yo, k4	35	
108	[WS] K4, purl to last 4 sts, k4	35	
109	[RS] K4, yo, k2tog, *p1, k1* to last 5 sts, k1, yo, k4	36	
110	[WS] K4, purl to last 4 sts, k4	36	
111	[RS] K4, yo, k2tog, knit to last 6 sts, ssk, yo, k4	36	
112	[WS] Knit all sts	36	
113	[RS] K4, yo, *k2tog, yo* to last 4 sts, k4	37	
114	[WS] Knit all sts	37	
115	[RS] K4, yo, k2tog, knit to last 6 sts, ssk, yo, k4	37	
116	[WS] K4, purl to last 4 sts, k4	37	
117	[RS] K4, yo, k2tog, *p1, k1* to last 5 sts, k1, yo, k4	38	
118	[WS] K4, purl to last 4 sts, k4	38	30%
119	[RS] K4, yo, k2tog, knit to last 6 sts, ssk, yo, k4	38	
120	[WS] Knit all sts	38	
121	[RS] K4, yo, *k2tog, yo* to last 4 sts, k4	39	

One Size

ROW	DIRECTIONS	TOTAL STITCHES	% DONE
122	[WS] Knit all sts	39	
123	[RS] K4, yo, k2tog, knit to last 6 sts, ssk, yo, k4	39	
124	[WS] K4, purl to last 4 sts, k4	39	
125	[RS] K4, yo, k2tog, *p1, k1* to last 5 sts, k1, yo, k4	40	
126	[WS] K4, purl to last 4 sts, k4	40	
127	[RS] K4, yo, k2tog, knit to last 6 sts, ssk, yo, k4	40	
128	[WS] Knit all sts	40	35%
129	[RS] K4, yo, *k2tog, yo* to last 4 sts, k4	41	
130	[WS] Knit all sts	41	
131	[RS] K4, yo, k2tog, knit to last 6 sts, ssk, yo, k4	41	
132	[WS] K4, purl to last 4 sts, k4	41	
133	[RS] K4, yo, k2tog, *p1, k1* to last 5 sts, k1, yo, k4	42	
134	[WS] K4, purl to last 4 sts, k4	42	
135	[RS] K4, yo, k2tog, knit to last 6 sts, ssk, yo, k4	42	
136	[WS] Knit all sts	42	
137	[RS] K4, yo, *k2tog, yo* to last 4 sts, k4	43	
138	[WS] Knit all sts	43	
139	[RS] K4, yo, k2tog, knit to last 6 sts, ssk, yo, k4	43	40%
140	[WS] K4, purl to last 4 sts, k4	43	
141	[RS] K4, yo, k2tog, *p1, k1* to last 5 sts, k1, yo, k4	44	
142	[WS] K4, purl to last 4 sts, k4	44	
143	[RS] K4, yo, k2tog, knit to last 6 sts, ssk, yo, k4	44	
144	[WS] Knit all sts	44	
145	[RS] K4, yo, *k2tog, yo* to last 4 sts, k4	45	
146	[WS] Knit all sts	45	
147	[RS] K4, yo, k2tog, knit to last 6 sts, ssk, yo, k4	45	
148	[WS] K4, purl to last 4 sts, k4	45	
149	[RS] K4, yo, k2tog, *p1, k1* to last 5 sts, k1, yo, k4	46	45%
150	[WS] K4, purl to last 4 sts, k4	46	
151	[RS] K4, yo, k2tog, knit to last 6 sts, ssk, yo, k4	46	

ROW	DIRECTIONS	TOTAL STITCHES	% DONE
152	[WS] Knit all sts	46	
153	[RS] K4, yo, *k2tog, yo* to last 4 sts, k4	47	
154	[WS] Knit all sts	47	
155	[RS] K4, yo, k2tog, knit to last 6 sts, ssk, yo, k4	47	
156	[WS] K4, purl to last 4 sts, k4	47	
157	[RS] K4, yo, k2tog, *p1, k1* to last 5 sts, k1, yo, k4	48	
158	[WS] K4, purl to last 4 sts, k4	48	
159	[RS] K4, yo, k2tog, knit to last 6 sts, ssk, yo, k4	48	50%
160	[WS] Knit all sts	48	
161	[RS] K4, yo, *k2tog, yo* to last 4 sts, k4	49	
162	[WS] Knit all sts	49	
163	[RS] K4, yo, k2tog, knit to last 6 sts, ssk, yo, k4	49	
164	[WS] K4, purl to last 4 sts, k4	49	
165	[RS] K4, yo, k2tog, *p1, k1* to last 5 sts, k1, yo, k4	50	
166	[WS] K4, purl to last 4 sts, k4	50	
167	[RS] K4, yo, k2tog, knit to last 6 sts, ssk, yo, k4	50	
168	[WS] Knit all sts	50	55%
169	[RS] K4, yo, *k2tog, yo* to last 4 sts, k4	51	
170	[WS] Knit all sts	51	
171	[RS] K4, yo, k2tog, knit to last 6 sts, ssk, yo, k4	51	
172	[WS] K4, purl to last 4 sts, k4	51	
173	[RS] K4, yo, k2tog, *p1, k1* to last 5 sts, k1, yo, k4	52	
174	[WS] K4, purl to last 4 sts, k4	52	
175	[RS] K4, yo, k2tog, knit to last 6 sts, ssk, yo, k4	52	
176	[WS] Knit all sts	52	
177	[RS] K4, yo, *k2tog, yo* to last 4 sts, k4	53	60%
178	[WS] Knit all sts	53	
179	[RS] K4, yo, k2tog, knit to last 6 sts, ssk, yo, k4	53	
180	[WS] K4, purl to last 4 sts, k4	53	
181	[RS] K4, yo, k2tog, *p1, k1* to last 5 sts, k1, yo, k4	54	

ROW	DIRECTIONS	TOTAL STITCHES	% DONE
182	[WS] K4, purl to last 4 sts, k4	54	
183	[RS] K4, yo, k2tog, knit to last 6 sts, ssk, yo, k4	54	
184	[WS] Knit all sts	54	65%
185	[RS] K4, yo, *k2tog, yo* to last 4 sts, k4	55	
186	[WS] Knit all sts	55	
187	[RS] K4, yo, k2tog, knit to last 6 sts, ssk, yo, k4	55	
188	[WS] K4, purl to last 4 sts, k4	55	
189	[RS] K4, yo, k2tog, *p1, k1* to last 5 sts, k1, yo, k4	56	
190	[WS] K4, purl to last 4 sts, k4	56	
191	[RS] K4, yo, k2tog, knit to last 6 sts, ssk, yo, k4	56	
192	[WS] Knit all sts	56	
193	[RS] K4, yo, *k2tog, yo* to last 4 sts, k4	57	70%
194	[WS] Knit all sts	57	
195	[RS] K4, yo, k2tog, knit to last 6 sts, ssk, yo, k4	57	
196	[WS] K4, purl to last 4 sts, k4	57	
197	[RS] K4, yo, k2tog, *p1, k1* to last 5 sts, k1, yo, k4	58	
198	[WS] K4, purl to last 4 sts, k4	58	
199	[RS] K4, yo, k2tog, knit to last 6 sts, ssk, yo, k4	58	
200	[WS] Knit all sts	58	75%
201	[RS] K4, yo, *k2tog, yo* to last 4 sts, k4	59	
202	[WS] Knit all sts	59	
203	[RS] K4, yo, k2tog, knit to last 6 sts, ssk, yo, k4	59	
204	[WS] K4, purl to last 4 sts, k4	59	
205	[RS] K4, yo, k2tog, *p1, k1* to last 5 sts, k1, yo, k4	60	
206	[WS] K4, purl to last 4 sts, k4	60	
207	[RS] K4, yo, k2tog, knit to last 6 sts, ssk, yo, k4	60	
208	[WS] Knit all sts	60	80%
209	[RS] K4, yo, *k2tog, yo* to last 4 sts, k4	61	
210	[WS] Knit all sts	61	
211	[RS] K4, yo, k2tog, knit to last 6 sts, ssk, yo, k4	61	

ROW	DIRECTIONS	TOTAL STITCHES	% DONE
212	[WS] K4, purl to last 4 sts, k4	61	
213	[RS] K4, yo, k2tog, *p1, k1* to last 5 sts, k1, yo, k4	62	
214	[WS] K4, purl to last 4 sts, k4	62	
215	[RS] K4, yo, k2tog, knit to last 6 sts, ssk, yo, k4	62	85%
216	[WS] Knit all sts	62	
217	[RS] K4, yo, *k2tog, yo* to last 4 sts, k4	63	
218	[WS] Knit all sts	63	
219	[RS] K4, yo, k2tog, knit to last 6 sts, ssk, yo, k4	63	
220	[WS] K4, purl to last 4 sts, k4	63	
221	[RS] K4, yo, k2tog, *p1, k1* to last 5 sts, k1, yo, k4	64	
222	[WS] K4, purl to last 4 sts, k4	64	90%
223	[RS] K4, yo, k2tog, knit to last 6 sts, ssk, yo, k4	64	
224	[WS] Knit all sts	64	
225	[RS] K4, yo, *k2tog, yo* to last 4 sts, k4	65	
226	[WS] Knit all sts	65	
227	[RS] Knit all sts	65	
228	[WS] Knit all sts	65	
229	[RS] Knit all sts	65	95%
230	[WS] Knit all sts	65	
231	[RS] Knit a s	65	
232	[WS] Knit all sts	65	
233	[RS] Knit all sts	65	
	Cast off: K1, *k1, transfer the 2 sts back to the left needle and k2tog through back loops,* repeat to end		100%

Yarn: The Fibre Co. Tundra

FINISHING

Weave in ends. Make and sew on tassels. See instructions on next page.

BLOCKING

For detailed blocking instructions see page 82.

MAKE TASSELS

1. Take a piece of thick card that is approximately 7.5cm / 3" wide (or however long you want your tassel to be) and wind your yarn around the card about 80-100 times or to the desired thickness of tassel.

2. Take a piece of yarn approximately 38cm / 15" long and thread it through the wound yarn, pull it tight and tie a knot at the top edge.

3. Once the top is secure, cut through the yarn at the bottom of the card.

4. Taking another piece of yarn, place the end beyond the bottom of the tassel (so you can easily find the right end later), loop it up above the point where you want the tie around the tassel to be and then wind the yarn around the tassel about 20 times.

5. To secure the end, take the yarn and thread it through the loop that is sticking out the top then gently pull the bottom of that thread down so the end is hidden underneath tassel binding.

6. Trim the ends of the tassel.

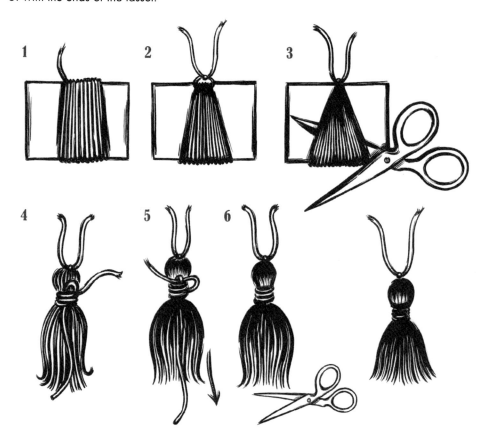

Abbreviations

CC	use contrast colour
k	knit
k2tog	knit two stitches together (1 st decreased)
k2tog tbl	knit two stitches together through the back loops (1 st decreased)
kfb	knit into front and back of stitch (1 st increased)
KSK	knit, slip, knit: Knit 1, slip 1 purlwise with yarn in front, knit 1
KYOK	k1, leaving stitch on left needle, yo, k1 into the same stitch (2 sts increased)
M1L	make 1 left. Insert left needle, from front to back, under strand of yarn which runs between next stitch on left needle and last stitch on right needle; knit this stitch through back loop (1 stitch increased)
M1R	make 1 right. Insert left needle, from back to front, under strand of yarn which runs between next stitch on left needle and last stitch on right needle; knit this stitch through front loop (1 stitch increased)
MC	use main colour
p	purl
p2tog	purl two stitches together (1 st decreased)
p2tog tbl	purl two stitches together through the back loops (1 st decreased)
PB	place bead — see techniques. If you are not using beads substitute K1 for PB in the pattern
PM	place marker
RS	right side
S2KP	slip 2 sts together knitwise, knit 1, pass slipped stitches over (2 sts decreased)
SKS	slip, knit, slip: Slip 1 purlwise with yarn in front, knit 1, slip 1 purlwise with yarn in front
sl1	slip one stitch as if to purl with yarn in back
sl1 wyf	slip 1 with yarn in front: bring yarn to the front, slip stitch purlwise, take yarn to back
SM	slip marker
ssk	slip 2 stitches, one at a time, knitwise, to the right needle; insert the left needle into the fronts of these two stitches and knit together (1 st decreased)
st(s)	stitch(es)
STAR	knit 3 stitches together without removing from left needle, yo, then knit those 3 stitches together again and remove from left needle
WS	wrong side
yo	yarn over (1 st increased)
*	repeat instructions between asterisks

Techniques

Using the Curious Handmade Percentage Checklist System™

I want to give you a personal introduction to the way I write my patterns. You may have noticed that The Shawl Society pattern format is a little bit different from traditional knitting patterns. That's because these are Curious Handmade Percentage Checklist Patterns™. So what is this all about, and how does it help?

Briefly, the Percentage Checklist is a visual way to chart your progress in the pattern and keep track of how much yarn you're using. I began using this method when I was designing shawls, but I quickly saw how useful it might be for knitters. On a whim, I decided to write up the pattern for one of my early shawls this way, and the feedback was astonishing. Everyone loved it, and I decided to make it a feature of my patterns.

Here's how it works:

First, weigh your yarn. You can use an ordinary kitchen scale or postage scale for this. If you're using off-the-shelf yarn it probably has a starting weight listed on the label, but if you're using homespun or leftover yarn from another project, don't skip this step!

Next, track your stitches. The column that says "Total Stitches" (see chart below) is your stitch count: the number of stitches you have on the needles after completing that row of the pattern. This makes it really easy to work out where you are up to in the pattern and helps to find mistakes quickly too. I like to keep track of rows with a pretty strip of washi tape, which I move down the page after each row.

Then, weigh your yarn as you go. The percentage complete column is based on the total number of stitches and it helps you to know if you will have enough yarn. For example, if you have reached the 50% complete row and have used less than half of your yarn then you know you are on track. You don't have to weigh after every row, but it's good to check in at certain milestones if you're not sure you have enough yarn. If it seems like your percentages are off by a lot, you may want to recheck your gauge.

ROW	DIRECTIONS	TOTAL STITCHES	% DONE
85	[RS]	255	50%
86	[WS]	257	
87	[RS]	261	
88	[WS]	263	
89	[RS]	267	55%
90	[WS]	269	

People also find the percentage system great to motivate them to finish their shawl. I think that's a lovely perk: something to help get you over the finish line! The Percentage Checklist has become a favourite feature for many of my knitters, and I hope you love it too.

ROW	DIRECTIONS	TOTAL STITCHES	% DONE
75	[RS]	225	
76	[WS]	227	40%
77	[RS] K3, KYOK, K9, *STAR, K3* to last 16 sts, STAR, K9, KYOK, k3	231	
78	[WS]	233	
79	[RS]	237	

Techniques
Blocking your Shawl

After all the knitting is done, there's one more step before your beautiful shawl is truly finished. In my opinion, blocking is one of the most magical parts of knitting. Stretching out your shawl to reveal its true beauty is a wonderful moment. All knitting benefits from blocking. The stitches open up and relax, the yarn fluffs up and "blooms" and the knitted fabric drapes beautifully once it dries. Lace especially looks so much better blocked, even simple eyelets. Here's how to make the magic happen!

BLOCKING - FIVE SIMPLE STEPS

Ingredient list:

- Yarn needle or darning needle with a large eye
- Bucket or sink
- Lukewarm water
- Baby shampoo or wool wash
- Large bath towel
- Pins
- Optional: blocking wires

You will also need a large flat area which can be pinned, like a foam mat or spare bed.

STEP 1

Weave in your ends. Once your shawl is complete, you'll have at least two dangling tails of yarn, one from when you cast on, and one from when you cast off. (If you used more than one skein of yarn to use different colours or make a larger shawl, you will have more tails to weave in).

To protect your shawl from unravelling and keep it strong, you need to weave those ends into your knitting.

There is no right or wrong way to weave in ends, as long as it's neat and you're happy with it. Make sure everything is nice and secure, but not too tight! You can wait to trim the last little bits of yarn tail until after you're finished blocking.

STEP 2

Fill a sink or bucket with lukewarm water. Don't use hot water: it can cause your yarn to felt. You can also add a tiny amount of a very mild shampoo, such as baby shampoo or a little wool wash.

STEP 3

Soak your shawl. Gently push your shawl under the water. Don't agitate the water too much, as the friction can also cause felting. Just gently press until the yarn has absorbed enough water to be fully saturated. Let it soak for 10 to 30 minutes.

If you used more than one colour in your shawl and you are worried about bleeding, stay on the shorter end of the soak time and check on it often. You might also want to add a little white vinegar to the soak. You can also buy "colour catcher" sheets to add to your soak which can help suck up any stray dye.

After soaking, you can rinse your shawl by emptying the bucket, refilling it with clean water (hold the shawl out of the way so that the agitation of the tap water doesn't hit it) and soaking again for a minute. Repeat as needed until the water runs clear.

STEP 4

The towel roll. Have a large towel laid out flat before you remove your shawl from the soak. Gently squeeze most of the water from your shawl: it's quite delicate at this moment, so it's important not to wring it or treat it roughly. Then, lay your shawl flat onto the bath towel, and start to roll the towel and the shawl together like a swiss roll, squeezing gently as you go, then unroll and check how wet the shawl is. You want it quite damp, but not dripping. If it's still very wet, repeat the towel roll with a dry towel.

STEP 5

Stretch. Lay your shawl out on your soft flat surface. You'll want to gently shape it into the desired final form of the shawl, whether that's a triangle or a gentle crescent. Once you have the general shape, you can start to stretch and pin. If you are using blocking wires, you'll generally want to start with a wire threaded through the top edge. If you are just using pins, start by finding and pinning the centre of the top edge. From there, just start gently pulling and pinning as you go. Keep adjusting and repinning as you go until you are happy with the shape of the shawl. Leave it to dry thoroughly. Once dry, if there are any little bits of ends left from your weaving in, snip them off.

- For crescent shawls: The ends of the top edge can be curved inwards into a soft "horseshoe" shape: this will make the shawl easier to wear.

- For a picot edge: You will want to pin each of the picots down individually to make them stand out.

Your yarn may react differently to blocking depending on what type of fibre you have used. Wool blends benefit from a lot of stretching, so don't be afraid to be firm. Luxury fibres, such as alpaca, cashmere, or silk may require a lighter touch. If you're in doubt, check with your yarn manufacturer.

All you need to do now is leave the shawl to dry and then enjoy your gorgeous new, finished object!

Techniques
Placing Beads

FOR THE PB ABBREVIATION

A beaded shawl makes a fabulous special occasion piece. When you add beads to a shawl you also add sparkle and a little extra weight. Beads catch the light beautifully and can also help a shawl knit from fine yarn drape better. Beading isn't difficult or complex, so don't be afraid to give it a try! There are several different techniques you can use to bead your knitting, but here's my favourite:

Note that PB counts as 1 stitch in the instructions.
The same stitch has a bead placed on it and is then knit. Some people prefer to place the bead and then slip the stitch and that is fine too.

1. Slip the bead onto the end of your crochet hook (over the hook).

2. Insert the hook into the stitch loop on the left needle, with the hook facing you.

3. Gently move the bead down over the hook onto the stitch.

4. Place the stitch back on the left needle.

5. Knit the stitch with the bead on it.

Deciding which yarn to use for a new shawl project is always one of the most exciting moments of the entire process. I had so much fun choosing yarns for all the Shawl Society Samples, and I know you will too.

Yarn
Choosing Yarns

I was lucky enough to work with some very wonderful yarn suppliers for The Shawl Society, and I highly recommend all of them. Of course, if you want to substitute another yarn from the one recommended in the pattern, that is absolutely allowed and encouraged! In fact, because I worked with so many indie dyers, you may discover that some of the colourways and bases those producers work with have evolved over time. It might not be possible to create an exact copy of the samples anymore, but I think there's something exciting about that. It's a prompt to indulge your own creativity and love of colour.

The information in this section provides some suggestions and guidance about types of yarn that might work for each shawl in the collection. If you'd like even more inspiration, I highly recommend a visit to Ravelry to see what other Shawl Society Members have chosen for their shawls.

Yarn
Choosing Yarns

YARN WEIGHT

The weight, or thickness, of your yarn is one of the most important considerations when you're choosing what to knit your shawl with. Choosing the right weight can be a bit of a challenge as the names and definitions of yarn weights can vary between countries and sometimes even between brands of yarn. The weights suggested in the patterns correspond to the yarns used for the samples.

SUBSTITUTING DIFFERENT YARN WEIGHTS

One of the wonderful things about shawl knitting is that you don't have to be exact about gauge or fit, so it's possible to use a different yarn weight if you have some stash you want to use or if you fall in love with something special in your local yarn shop. If you decide to do this, you may need to change your needles and the total amount of yarn. A change in yarn weight and needle size can affect the size of the finished shawl: a lighter weight yarn on smaller needles will result in a smaller shawl, while using a heavier weight yarn and larger needles will mean a bigger shawl. Stating the obvious perhaps, but something to keep in mind.

Very often the label on a skein (or the online listing) will give a recommended gauge for the yarn. It can give you a general idea of how big a difference there is between the yarn you're considering and the recommended weight. It is probably easiest to stay within one degree of difference. So, for example, if you want to substitute yarn for a shawl that's written for fingering weight, it would be easiest to either go down to lace or up to sport or DK weight.

Here's a quick rundown of the yarn weights used in this collection.

Asana

Lace weight

One of the Asana samples uses a lace weight yarn, also referred to as 2-ply. Lace weight yarn makes beautiful fabric for light, yet still very warm shawls.

Talisman, Asana, Amulet, Aurorae

Fingering weight

Fingering weight yarn is also referred to as sock weight or 4-ply. I love using this weight of yarn for shawls because it is light enough to create delicate, lacy effects, but sturdy enough to stand up to everyday wear. It is thicker and knits up faster than lace weight, but is thin enough to offer a softer drape than a heavier weight yarn.

Aurorae

Sport Weight

One of the Aurorae samples uses a sport weight yarn, also sometimes referred to as 5-ply. Sport weight has a lovely substantial feel to the fabric.

Quill

DK weight

The DK stands for double knitting, or 8-ply and this yarn weight is extremely versatile. Thicker than fingering and sport but still relatively lightweight, it is hugely popular and strikes a great balance between drapey and cuddly

Sonder

Bulky

This heavyweight yarn goes by different names depending on where you live: often known as bulky, chunky or 12-ply. There are two huge advantages to using such a thick yarn. First, it makes for an incredibly squishy and cosy finished object. Second, it knits up super, super fast!

FIBRE CONTENT

Yarns made of different fibres may not act the same on the needles and will feel different against your skin. For a shawl that you plan to wear around your neck, something soft like merino, cashmere, or alpaca is very luxurious. I find blends with a bit of luxury fibre and some wool for strength and warmth work very well. Silk is gorgeous but can be a little bit slippery and tricky by itself, especially if you are a beginner. Linen, bamboo, or cotton will make a wonderful summery wrap but these yarns don't have the same spring and flexibility of wool and may also be more challenging fibres for a beginner.

SOLID COLOUR, TONAL & VARIEGATED YARN

Knitters often wonder whether or not they should use variegated yarns to knit their Shawl Society Patterns. As you can see from the photographs in the book, I used a wide range of different types of colourways for the samples.

Some variegated yarns have a reputation for obscuring detailed lace or stitch patterns. It's a matter of personal taste: I think a gently variegated yarn can look really beautiful in lace, but many knitters prefer to use a solid or tonal colourway for those sections.
If you haven't knitted much with variegated yarns, the effects some of them create can be a bit of a surprise. Striping, flashing, or pooling can happen with long colour repeats: you may love this look or you may want to avoid it. Randomly dyed yarn can give you a more speckled effect. I think gentle speckled yarns often give you the best of both worlds!

Above all, let yourself be guided by whatever makes you happy while you're knitting it and when you're wearing it. That's the true beauty of handmade things: it's all about your own taste.

Yarn
Featured Yarns

TALISMAN

The Wool Kitchen
Urban Hints

When I met Helen Reed, the indie dyer behind the Wool Kitchen, at the Edinburgh Yarn Festival, my magpie-like attraction to beautifully coloured yarn went into overdrive! I couldn't resist her yarns and I cast on the first shawl for The Shawl Society on the way home from the festival.

Helen hand dyes her yarn with lots of love and attention in her studio in London and is a one-woman indie business like me. This yarn is produced in small quantities, and Helen has regular yarn updates in her Etsy shop.

www.thewoolkitchen.com

Northbound Knitting
BFL Silk Fingering

Northbound Knitting is by indie dyer and designer Lisa Mutch who is based in Canada. I used 2 skeins of the NBK BFL/Silk fingering for the medium and large sizes but you can also use 1 skein for the small size if you wish. The colours are so dreamy and perfect for an indulgent soft shawl to wrap around your shoulders. The yarn base is made for shawls...Blue Faced Leicester is a strong, sleek yet soft fibre and the silk adds a wonderful sheen and drape to the shawl.

www.northboundknitting.com/

AMULET

Seven Sisters Arts
Matrika

Karen is a brilliant indie yarn dyer from the beautiful state of Maine. I first met her at the Knitting Pipeline Georgia retreat. She is personally delightful and so creatively talented, and of course, I was captured right away by the magic of her yarn. This particular base is something very special. The sheen of the silk combined with Karen's uncanny knack for colour makes the skeins so luminous that they almost seem to glow under the light. You can buy this gorgeous yarn at the Seven Sisters Arts website, and they ship internationally.

www.sevensistersarts.com

Madelinetosh
Tosh Merino Light

This yarn is an old favourite for me. It's exquisite to work with, and the wonderful stitch definition lends itself to lace shawls. The colour I used is full of rich golden tones, a warm earthy neutral but with a glamorous sheen. It has sadly been discontinued, but I know you'll fall instantly in love with one (or more) of the many beautiful current colours. I find them all irresistible.

www.madelinetosh.com

Yarn
Featured Yarns

ASANA

The Uncommon Thread
Tough Sock

Don't let the name fool you: while this is a hardwearing yarn, it is still gorgeously soft and elegant. Cosy and gentle against the skin, it has a lovely drape. The Uncommon Thread produces wonderful hand-dyed artisan yarns with a huge and sophisticated palette that ranges from whispery hints of colour, to deep, saturated jewel tones. They are devoted to environmentally friendly production, which makes it easier to stash their beautiful yarn without guilt.

www.theuncommonthread.co.uk

Eden Cottage Yarn
Theseus Lace (discontinued and now called Titus Lace)

I am a huge fan of Eden Cottage Yarn, which is hand-dyed in small batches in a West Yorkshire studio. Victoria is the magical dyer behind their signature muted palette of semi-solid shades. There is so much romance in these colours, and the fact that she dyes with an eye to sustainability makes them even more beautiful to me. This base is incredibly soft and smooth, with just enough silk to give a glow and sheen to the yarn without making it difficult to handle.

www.edencottageyarns.co.uk

QUILL

Blacker Yarn
Tamar DK

Tamar is a unique yarn, made from a special class of sheep. Lustre wools from these British rare breeds have a natural shimmer and glow that has to be seen to be believed. The added Cornish Mule content gives the yarn a bouncy, cushy body, and it comes from local lambs, so it is still beautifully soft. I'm a big admirer of Blacker Yarns in general. I've had them on the podcast more than once to talk about small batch British wool. I love what they do, the way they do it, and the passion they put into every yarn they produce.

www.blackeryarns.co.uk

Yarn
Featured Yarns

AURORAE

Copper Corgi
Gradient Mini Skein Set

Sarah of The Copper Corgi is a world-class indie dyer in Savannah Georgia. I met her at my first Knitting Pipeline Georgia retreat and I had been wanting to design a shawl with this breathtaking gradient for such a long time. She has such an eye for rich colours and evocative combinations.

www.etsy.com/shop TheCopperCorgi

Seven Sisters Arts
Meridian Gradient Set

Seven Sisters Arts is an established indie yarn company founded by Karen Grover and their fibres and yarns are carefully chosen with the provenance and the end product in mind. Ever since I met Karen at the Knitting Pipeline retreat, I've been a huge fan. This particular set had me enchanted from the moment I laid eyes on it, and the evocative colour names just add to its mystique.

Karen also created a second, lighter version of this colourway and named it Aurora, in honour of this shawl. At time of printing, it is still available to purchase from the Seven Sisters Arts website!

www.sevensistersarts.com

SONDER

The Fibre Co
Tundra

I am such a fan of The Fibre Co. and any chance to design with their stunning yarns is a wonderful treat for me. There's so much thought and creativity in every yarn they release. Tundra is a wonderful example of the craftsmanship and luxury for which the Fiber Co. is known. A big cloud of alpaca and merino of intense softness, and a sheen of silk for a special glow, it feels incredible to knit with and to wear.

You can find your nearest Tundra stockist on The Fibre Co.'s Retailer page.

www.thefibreco.com

Thank you to the companies who provided yarn support for the patterns in this book.

Choosing Needles and other supplies

For shawl knitting, a circular needle with a long cable (100 cm) makes everything much easier. We are not knitting "in the round" with these. Instead, we knit back and forth like you would on straight needles. The cord is used to hold the large number of stitches that are created as the shawl grows.

When you buy your yarn, you may notice a "suggested needle size" printed on the ball band. For shawl projects, where we are creating an open, drapey fabric, you'll usually want to use a slightly larger needle than is recommended on the yarn's label. I give recommended needle sizes for each shawl pattern, but depending on the gauge your perfect size may be different.

The material and sharpness of your needles will change your knitting experience.

- Extra-sharp lace needles can make it a little easier to work with a fine yarn when you are knitting lace or twisted stitch patterns.
- Wooden or bamboo needles tend to grip the yarn a little more. This can slow knitting down, but that's not a bad thing if you're knitting with a slippery fibre like silk.
- If you're looking for speed, metal or carbon needles are smoother and slicker, so that the yarn slides on and off the needles quickly. This is great if you've got a rhythm going and like to knit fast, but can be a little tricky for new knitters or when combined with slippery yarns.

BEADS

If you love beads you might have something in your stash to suit. If you're shopping for beads online try Etsy. Look for "seed" beads as they usually have a bigger hole than for jewellery. If you use the crochet hook method to add beads you'll need a US Steel Size 12/1.0mm Crochet hook (or hook small enough to fit through holes in beads).

Notes

About

Helen Stewart lives in London, where she spends her days designing knitting patterns and hosting the award-winning Curious Handmade podcast. She was inspired to start the Shawl Society because she believes that making things by hand really is magical, and she's seen how much that magic is multiplied when you can share the experience with other people. Obsessed with clarity, detail, and proportion in all of her designs, she creates beautiful patterns which are straightforward enough for everyone to achieve but challenging enough to be addictive. Helen loves to combine knitting with her other passions; travel, photography, and meeting up with knitters from around the world.

For

My husband, Steve and my little muses Sophie and Lexie
who make me want to be the best I can be.

Thank you

To my knitters Deb Hickman, Fiona Hobson,
Tracey Reavell-Roy and Pauline Wall

To my technical and copy editor Emma James

To my copywriter Amanda Gareis
for your beautiful descriptions

To Vicki Hillman for photography

To Paula Emons-Fuessle for all
your encouragement

THE

Shawl Society

SEASON 1

Six shawl knitting patterns to delight and inspire

Free Bonus Videos

Bonus videos are available from:

www.curioushandmade.com/TSS1Bonus

I share tutorials for techniques used in the patterns, as well as an introduction to the shawls where I talk about the inspiration and behind the scenes of designing the shawls.

Be Social

Join in the conversation and knit alongs on:

☐ www.instagram.com/curioushandmade/

☐ www.facebook.com/CuriousHandmade/

© www.ravelry.com/groups/curious-handmade